AF344786

RETHINKING ECCLESIA

Being and Becoming Christ Communities:
Towards a Borderless Church

Empowerment, Educational, Health,
Healing and Harmony Perspectives

RETHINKING ECCLESIA

Being and Becoming Christ Communities: Towards a Borderless Church

Empowerment, Educational, Health, Healing and Harmony Perspectives

EDITORS

Daniel Rathnakara Sadananda

Solomon Paul J.

CHURCH OF SOUTH INDIA
2021

Rethinking Ecclesia – Being and Becoming Christ Communities: Towards a Borderless Church – Empowerment, Educational, Health, Healing and Harmony Perspectives - Jointly Published by the Indian Society for Promoting Christian Knowledge (ISPCK), Post Box 1585, Kashmere Gate, Delhi-110006 and The Church of South India (CSI), CSI Centre, No. 5, Whites Road, Royapettah, Chennai – 600 014.

© CSI, 2021

All rights reserved. No part of this book may be reproduced or transmitted in any form or by any means, electronic, mechanical, photocopying, recording, or by any information storage and retrieval system, without the prior permission in writing from the publisher.

The views expressed in the book are those of the author and the publisher takes no responsibility for any of the statements.

Online Order: http://ispck.org.in/book.php

ISBN: 978-93-90569-16-8

Laser typeset by

ISPCK, Post Box 1585, 1654, Madarsa Road, Kashmere Gate, Delhi-110006 • *Tel:* 23866323

e-mail: ashish@ispck.org.in • ella@ispck.org.in
website: www.ispck.org.in

Contents

Acknowledgements

Rethinking Ecclesia publication is a result of well thought and planned series of 8 consultations in the year 2018. These consultations are indeed a historical moment in the history of CSI as we commemorated 70 years of faithful journey and Reformation 500. All the papers presented and the meaningful conversations helped the Church of South India to engage more vigorously in the process of searching new theological directions and visions as CSI steps into a new decade.

The theme "Being and becoming Christ communities – towards a borderless Church" were discussed from a) Biblical perspective, b) theological and ethical perspective, c) liturgical and missiological perspective, d) prophetic and diaconal perspective, e) empowerment and educational perspective, f) healing and reconciliation perspective, g)National and global ecumenical perspective.

The Moderator of the Church of South India, Most Rev Thomas K Oommen, who inaugurated these consultations, remarked that the theological exercise of Rethinking Ecclesia consultations has helped the Church to find new directions in the pilgrim journey of CSI. He said that these explorations should continue to challenge the church and its mission and also make way for newer forms of ministerial engagements with the people at the grassroots.

These consultations has enabled the church to make a theological audit of CSI, create a network of theological educators who are CSI and gave opportunity for the seminary and the church to bridge the existing gaps in working closely with one another for the sake of a united mission.

This book is a compilation of articles presented during the Biblical and Theological perspective consultations held at CSI Synod, Chennai. Biblical scholars and theologians of CSI came and presented their insights on the theme.

At this moment we thank the God of koinoinia who called CWM to partner with CSI from the beginning till the end of this Rethinking Ecclesia consultations helping us to encourage each other and also assuring us of God's accompaniment in our Pilgrim journey.

I also place my thanks to the Youth Department of CSI for their meticulous efforts in planning and implementation of these consultations and coordination in bringing out this publication.

Special thanks to ISPCK for publishing these books and partnering with CSI in continuance of God's mission.

Rathnakara Sadananda

Preface

It is with great joy and contentment that I present the book – **Rethinking Ecclesia: Being and Becoming Christ Communities - Towards a borderless Church**, a series of articles deliberating on the theme from Biblical and Theological perspectives.

Borders have become an undeniable reality today. Both the nation-state and the Church are governed by borders. If borders are to offer security and protection, the same borders also exclude or de-mark the other. The Church in India, since many decades now has been struggling to engage with the many identity-markers such as caste, region, denomination, tradition, gender and so on… Though the Church is called to live and profess the liberating Spirit of God which transcends borders yet, she is engaged in grappling with the many challenges imposed by the identity-markers.

These identity-markers which promote intrinsic value to the worth of an individual and betterment of the community have become a strong border/barrier among communities leading to negation of life. It is in this context that the book "Rethinking Ecclesia" tries to find meaning and sense for the existence of the CSI today and tomorrow.

The articles in this book resonate the visions, dreams, aspirations and even frustrations in re-imaging a new community centered on Christ and show the way forward towards a borderless Church. These articles are not ashamed of the grave mistakes the Church has committed in stiffening borders and building walls of animosity, but have rather lamented over them in repentance, waiting for another opportunity to set it right through theological articulations. They reflect on the present context of the Church battling even more greater hurdles as the socio-geo-political climate of the nation is going through a shift towards rightist ideological forces.

"**Rethinking Ecclesia**" is the result of a well-thought and planned series of eight consultations in the year 2018. These consultations were indeed a historical moment in the history of CSI as we commemorated 70 years of faithful journey and Reformation 500. All the papers presented, and the meaningful conversations helped the Church of South India to engage more vigorously in the process of searching for new theological directions and visions as the CSI steps into a new decade.

The theme "**Being and becoming Christ communities – towards a borderless Church**" were discussed from a) Biblical, b) Theological, c) Liturgical and Missiological, d) Prophetic Diaconal, e) Empowerment and Educational, f) Health, Healing and Harmony as well as g) National and Global Ecumenical perspectives. Around 109 papers were presented during these consultations containing voices from within and outside, voices of complement and voices of dissent, voices from the vulnerable and those in responsible positions.

The Moderator of the Church of South India, Most Rev Thomas K. Oommen, who inaugurated these consultations, remarked that the theological exercise of Rethinking Ecclesia consultations has helped the Church to find new directions in the pilgrim journey of CSI. He said that these explorations should continue to challenge the Church and its mission and also make way for newer forms of ministerial engagements with the people at the grassroots, especially in liberating the weak and the oppressed.

These consultations affirmed that the Church is the sign and the sacrament of the reign of God; that as the continuation of the incarnation and an instrument of the reign of God, the Church ventures to live out her commitment and faith as an alternative, that proclaims boldly that another world is possible, right here and now in our midst; and that the Church is the penultimate, subject to change and transformation till she is ultimately absorbed into the very reign of God. And therefore, the consultations were indeed a prophetic call to rethink *ecclesia*, not only its significance, importance and relevance, but also its being and becoming.

These consultations have enabled the Church to make a theological audit of CSI, create a network of theological educators in the CSI and provide opportunity for the theological faculties and the Church to bridge the existing gaps in working closely with one another for the sake of a united mission. Consultations also provided the much-needed space for the Church and the theological fraternity to listen to, have dialogue with one another, and work together to overcome the lacuna that exists between the seminary and the sanctuary.

This book is a compilation of articles presented during the consultations from **Empowerment, Educational, Healing and Harmony Perspectives** held at CSI Synod, Chennai. Educationists, doctors, counsellors and theologians of CSI came and presented their insights on the theme. The opinions and theological assertions expressed in the articles are of the authors themselves, put forth with sincere faith and hope that they would help the people of God to clearly and relevantly articulate the self-understanding of being and becoming Ecclesia.

Heartfelt thanks to the Moderator of CSI, Rt. Rev. Thomas K. Oommen, Deputy Moderator, Rt. Rev. V. Prasada Rao, and Treasurer, Adv. C. Robert Bruce for their immense solidarity and leadership during all the consultations that took place. Special thanks to the General Secretary, Rev. Dr. Daniel Rathnakara Sadananda, who was responsible for this theological exploration and exercise, without whose guidance these consultations and this publication would not have been possible.

We thank the God of *koinoinia* who called the CWM to partner with CSI from the beginning till the end of these "Rethinking Ecclesia" consultations by helping us to encourage each other and also assuring us of God's accompaniment in our pilgrim journey towards becoming a borderless Church.

I also place my thanks to Mrs. Augustina Margaret, staff, Youth Department, CSI for her efforts in planning and implementation of these consultations and for coordinating to bring out this publication. Thanks to Mrs. Jessica Richard and Mrs. Angel Merlin for their help in proof reading and special thanks to ISPCK for publishing these books and partnering with CSI in the continuance of God's mission.

Epiphany, 2020   **Solomon Paul J.**
Chennai, India   **Editor**

Towards a Borderless Church

At the time of independence in August 1947, the colonial masters re-drew the borders of our nation even as it wriggled in pain and tension. People began to move to safer places, many were displaced from their habitats and lives and livelihoods lost. The country paid dearly for its independence. In September 1947, our fore-fathers and mothers decided to overcome the borders of denominational faith, mission allegiance and regionalism to form the Church of South India. Inspired by the Lord's prayer for unity and oneness 'that they all may be one as we are one', our fore-fathers and mothers ventured into a radical discipleship of imitating God's oneness. To a divided India, to the divided church worldwide, the Church of South India became a parable of unity, a beacon of hope, an aroma of the Gospel.

Borders do exist. Each cell in our body has a border. However, each cell communicates and interacts with the other. Every one of us lives within certain borders and ever-widening borders, within the borders of our home, family, congregation, faith communities, village, town, state, and country. At times we share borders, we cross borders, we merge borders, we re-draw borders. We dream of borderless-ness. Thus, we live with borders, yet we yearn for borderless-ness. In our quest to understand borders and borderless-ness, we learn to understand the energy, power, potentials and the possibilities and opportunities that evolve in crossing and going beyond our borders.

A borderless Church calls us to look intently at our borders. Normally, borders are identity markers. Borders do inform us about what we are and what we are becoming. Anglican, Presbyterian, Congregationalist, and Methodist Christians in Southern India decided to redraw their ecclesial borders together to form, very consciously, a united and uniting Church of national and cultural identity. They indeed looked intently on the form of their faith, spiritual expressions, traditions, spiritual practice and how they organised themselves as congregations and churches. The varied faith expressions, spirituality, and liturgical traditions mingled together in their many-ness, yet interwoven into a colourful and powerful expression of oneness. The borders merged, were redrawn, new borders emerged.

In the first creation story, borderless-ness and harmony are evident. The varied, multiple forms and creatures created multitudes of borders that were held together in oneness and wholeness, an intrinsically connected, networked, harmonious blend is seen as good, and very good, culminating in Sabbath, the Shalom. Only the second creation story speaks of the process of self-discovery in relation to the other - in holding the other in respect and dignity, the identity of each is defined, interpreted and enhanced. The concept of identity formation, freedom with responsibility is introduced in the narrative only to affirm that when identity is misrepresented, and when the creature tries to impersonate the Creator, the connections, bonds and networks get destroyed.

The call and election narratives in the Old Testament are an invitation to understand this complex, yet beautiful interrelatedness and intrinsic value. The narratives of Abraham, Sarah and Hagar, Isaac and Rebecca, Esau, Jacob, Leah and Rachel show that they are invited to cross borders, share borders, draw new borders, and understand the mysteries beyond their borders and become a borderless community. For the writers of Genesis, their histories inform us of God's initiative that challenges human community to rediscover, reinvent and remember the borderless creation and be part of God's Shalom.

The story of Exodus is about breaking the borders that exploit and are oppressive. It is a story of empowerment for liberation; crossing the red sea - a baptism in water, is the visual symbol of overcoming borders and becoming a liberated community, a parable of liberation. The liberated community was called to represent the possibility of another world, where the world can hear its breathing and visualise its being. The commandments and the book of the covenant were given in order to make an alternative, another world possible, it was drawing new borders that would negate the borders that exploit, oppress, destroy and threaten life and proclaim the coming of justice and peace, not only within the borders of the liberated community, but beyond its borders and everywhere. Love, faithfulness, peace, justice, and righteousness are to be seen and experienced within the liberated community in order that it becomes the Gospel to the whole world.

The Deuteronomic eucharistic prayer (*anamnesis* - Deut. 26:5-10) holds together the wandering Aramean walking from the margins, crossing borders, the small and insignificant, few and negligible, strangers and aliens becoming empowered, to go through the struggles, pains, and sufferings, getting liberated from the crushing clutches of death and destruction to emerge as a people. It is a narration of resilience and resurrection, a living experience of breaking the chains of bondage and enslavement, to redraw borders that seem to extend and expand unceasingly.

The Prophetic literature which came at the time of exilic and post exilic period clearly depicts the community that was called to be an alternative, liberated community, which by losing its way and its borders emerged from its struggles of being conquered and occupied. The prophetic voice makes it clear that when the community loses its vision of liberation, corruption and injustice extinguish the power to move, connect and be open, when the community loses its dynamism and becomes static; connectivity, networks, and the power to transcend are destroyed and in the process people get marginalised and lose the creative power to overcome the borders and transcend the borders. Therefore, the prophetic call comes first as comforting, then as sowing the vision of a new heaven and new earth, but with a strong inclination to empower the community against corruption, injustice, oppression, and exploitation, so that they may discern and embrace the new that is already there and sprouting. Only in empowering the marginalised, in drawing out the inherent, innate, and immanent potentials, does the community once again regain movement, connectivity, and openness.

In the New Testament, Jesus' understanding of God as is defined in his conversation with the Samaritan woman is very instructive and profound - "God is Spirit; those who worship him must worship him in Spirit and truth" (Jn.4.24). God does not belong to one community, he is not stationary at Jerusalem or in Shechem, on the mount; God cannot be bound to certain traditions and forms of spirituality; he is boundless and borderless.

Jesus was preaching the reign of God, its imminence, and the reign of God, not the Church, was at the centre of his teaching. The reign of God is the safe space, that comforts, cares, heals and reconciles. It is a place where one receives forgiveness, grace, and loving kindness. The reign of God is where one rests powerlessness, vulnerability, frailty, weakness, insufficiency, and gets empowered. The reign of God calls the excluded, rejected, oppressed and outcastes, embraces them into an inclusive solidarity, to offer justice and peace. The reign of God is love, joy and hope, that brings integrity, wholeness, and harmony. It is the space and place where people experience the presence and accompaniment of God. The reign of God that Jesus proclaimed therefore, is not only borderless, but that which also gives assurance of eternity.

To make God's reign felt and experienced by commoners, Jesus' movement was evolved within the borders of Jewish religion. Jesus called out (*ecclesia*) twelve/seventy and created a community within the community. On this rock, I will build my Church (Matt.16.18), a rock-like, solid faith; but unlike the traditional understandings of messianic liberation, redemption was brought about by the suffering servant. Jesus standing firmly on the prophetic traditions of his faith, practiced prophetic *diakonia* as the means and instrument of liberation (Matt.16:21,24,25). Indeed, this was the culmination of a borderless, prophetic diaconal movement that moved from Nazareth to Gennesaret, to Tire Sidon, Samaria and to Jerusalem and back to Galilee. A borderless movement that empowered the margins, resisted the empire, critiqued religion and embraced the marginalised. It was a community called to be salt and light; a new life-giving and life-affirming movement, as flowing water and wind that blows wherever it pleases, a borderless new creation.

The Evangelists interpreted the crucified Christ as the one who draws all people to himself as he is lifted up. The crucified one, broken, crushed, and eliminated signifies the movement of the crucified people, and draws together those who are condemned to margins, denied of space, opportunity, rights and honour, bound because of their innocence and ignorance, excluded, made voiceless and unjustly persecuted. The crucified one in his passion and death enters the crucified communities and releases the power of life. The resurrected one who is boundless, and has overcome the limitations of time and space, inaugurates a new creation, boundless and borderless.

The early Church was indeed borderless, as it understood Jesus' command to go and make disciples of all nations (Matt.29:19), as a mandate to create borderless Christ communities. It also had a clear geographical strategy, 'you will be witnesses, in Jerusalem and in all Judea and Samaria and to the ends of the earth' (Acts 1:8). Peter also is 'converted' to the borderless Church, after the vision and real-life experience at Joppa and Caesarea (Acts 10). Paul, after his world-encircling, missional engagements writes his faith conviction; his *magna carta* "there is neither Jew nor Greek, slave nor free, male or female for you are all one in Christ" (Gal.3:28). It is very consistent with his sacramental theology which envisions a borderless Church, "Do you not know that all of us who have been baptized into Christ Jesus were baptized into his death? Therefore, we have been buried with him by baptism into death, so that, just as Christ was raised from the dead by the glory of the Father, so we too might walk in newness of life" (Rom.6:3,4). Every follower of Christ has been baptized into Christ, and therefore when he writes to Corinthians he clarifies that "The bread that we break, is it not a sharing in the body of Christ? Because there is one bread, we who are many are one body, for we all partake of the one bread" (1 Cor.10:16,17).

The ecclesiological reflections in the letter of Hebrews speaks of the visible and invisible Church. The language that 'we are surrounded by a great cloud of witnesses' (Heb.12:1), connects us with the Church of yesterday, with the Church of today and the future. The language used in the catholic epistles, of being strangers and pilgrims, to reflect the nature and being of the Church, depicts the struggles of living up to the great vision of a people of God. The theological affirmation that the Church is the Household of God (Eph.2:19) compared to the households of the time, and of the Church as God's House inform us about the profound theological affirmation: "Once you were not a people, now you are the people of God" (1Pet.2:10).

The eschatological vision of the book of Revelation depicts the New Jerusalem, the space of peace as an inclusive space, without borders. It speaks about a most valuable, yet fully transparent space, a space without a temple, as the whole space itself has the presence of God, which is light. All the nations of the earth will bring their splendor into it, it has gates that will always remain open, yet nothing impure will enter it (Rev.21:22ff). Even the heavenly space is not static; it is dynamic and transforming. The river of water of life, as clear as crystal flowing from the throne of God, and the trees of life which are for the healing and reconciliation of the nations, clearly affirm the process of being and becoming a Christ community, a borderless Church.

Today, we understand the Church as a sign and sacrament of the reign of God. She is an instrument of the reign of God and alternative that proclaims that another world is possible, that it is here and now in our midst. The Church is the penultimate, subject to change and transformation till she is absorbed into the reign of God. As a sign and sacrament of the reign of God, the Church has distinctive, discernible identity markers and borders, yet calling and exhorting people to the borderless reign of God.

As the Church of South India steps into the eighth decade of her being and becoming, may she be given grace upon grace to understand anew the gift of oneness and unity. May the 70-year celebrations be a sign of prophetic SEVA (*diakonia*), Social Empowerment - a Vision in Action upholding the sacramentality of life, where she, as a borderless Church travels beyond suspicion, fear and hostility in a multi-religious, multi-lingual, multi-cultural society. May she be empowered and emboldened to share, cross and redraw borders in order to set the energy of the margins, the crucified peoples free. May the children and the young be inspired to DARE into a process of Discernment And Radical Engagement, and be change makers and signs of transformation. May she be given grace to be a real MITHRA (friend) - Migrant Intervention Towards Holistic Responsive Action, to understand the beauty and significance of the small, frail and vulnerable, and be a movement of protest and resistance that gives DISHA, a new direction (Disability Intervention for Solidarity and Holistic Accompaniment), for those disabled, excluded, and condemned to margins. May the Church of South India be given grace to be God's instrument that brings dynamism and moves people, to connect not only with the Creator, but also with those around and all of God's creation, to open new possibilities of celebrating and living life in all its fulness. May the Church of South India be a new GEET, song (Gender Equity and Enabling Timetable), harmony that proclaims and practices equality, justice, and peace. In being and becoming a borderless Church, may the Church of South India open herself to God's eschaton, move in her radical engagement in the ever-continuous movement of unity and oneness of all and experience the fullness of Him who fills everything in every way (Eph.1:22), so that God may be all in all (1 Cor.15:28).

Rev. Dr. D. Rathnakara Sadananda
General Secretary, CSI

1

Education:
Pursuit of Alternative Ideas and Imaginations

Daniel Ezhilarasu

Introduction

The process of education is as old as humanity. Education leads to civilized people where values can be inculcated through the process of teaching and learning. I am sure all of us agree that education is defined as the source of edification. The efforts initiated by the Church of South India to urge the people of God to take stock of its ministry as it commemorates Reformation 500 and CSI 70 years is laudable. We need to acknowledge the contributions of the church and its institutions including institutes of higher education in knowledge creation and application to transform in order to enjoy God's creation. Our forefathers considered education as an instrument to realize one's vision. However, there are certain misconceptions and traditions that bound the institutions which hurdle their mission and creative engagement.

One of the foundational understandings is that Jesus Christ came to this world to save everyone. All the four gospel books proclaim that Jesus's kingdom is not only borderless but it also promises the blessings of eternity. The movement started by Jesus is not for one community or a religion. Jesus encouraged people differently. There was a marked shift in Jesus' understanding of the context and its praxis.

Alternative Ideas and Imaginations – Fostering Creativity and Free-Thinking

According to Covey, 'If we do the same things in the same way, we get the same result'. It is vital that we think alternative methods in education in order to get results that are innovative and creative. Education is primarily creating ideas which involves imagination. Real learning encourages learners to think out of the box. Search and research should help in solving many of the issues faced by humanity. Human beings are created in the image of God and are endowed with the power of being creative, innovating new ideas and being spontaneous in action.

Creativity can be redefined as the capacity to grow to one's fullest potential and survive in a competitive environment. A perfect educational ambience encourages learners to question and challenge the core assumptions marking a radical breakthrough and coming up with new assumptions. Creativity comes from within and not from outside. Every situation has the potential to be altered and improved creatively. Intuition with the right blend of logical thinking become the basis of creativity. We can move beyond barriers and obstacles only when we think differently. The contemporary challenges are of such magnitude that only collective thinking and concerted effort can get us out of the burning issues. At this point, it is pertinent that we as children of God, the liberator, ponder over the question - Do we really provide opportunity for the people of God to think creatively? Creativity is not inborn. Everyone can be creative. Do we nurture it?

It is wrong to construe that imagination is a forte of the lazy. People perish where there is no vision and vision are a divine intervention. An individual's vision can be realized through corporate efforts.

Alternative ideas of the people or believers need to be acceptable for the sake of helping the individuals, institutions and the larger church to fulfill the divine mandate. Free- thinking need not be wild but must be characterized and conditioned by the word of God.

The Context of the Church

We live in a fragmented world, torn apart by racial and cultural prejudices, and insensitivity towards the less privileged. It is amidst these conflicting values and life style that the church is called to serve the world as a moral community rooted in the justice of God. The task of the church is to identify, name and overthrow the forces that destroy fullness of life for all. An attitude, ideology or an inherited pattern of life can act as a barrier, which may try to defeat the power of love. Jesus wants us to look critically and creatively at our inherited attitudes, teachings and structures, which violate the demands of divine justice for all. Furthermore, Jesus wants us to visualize the creation of a just order for today and tomorrow.

Courage to Change

As we look closely into the life of the Church, we could identify forces like casteism, racism, ethnicity that impair the flow of authentic life. The Jews divided human society into two blocks namely Jews and Gentiles. Greeks divided the world into Greeks and Barbarians, and similarly, all decisions were made based on religion and caste. Presently, the challenge before the church is the evolution of a new humanity; where we are called to welcome one another as Christ welcomed us.

Marginalization of the people is a threat to the Church where the less privileged are deprived of their physical and spiritual resources of the poor. In the globalized world, the church should not look at issues as how the world looks at it. Walls built or erected between the haves and the have-nots should be broken down. People should be made to realize the language of compassion which is the cementing force for nation building. In other words, the culture of violence needs to be replaced by the culture of peace.

Action Plan: How to translate these concepts into concrete and desirable actions?

The church, which has a major challenge of providing education to the people (including children, youth and adults) need to draw a plan to make education as the key instrument of action in every walk of life. The education need not be confined only to schools and colleges, but it is always necessary that education take place in all places.

How and to whom can we focus?

1. **Children:** The church should address and inculcate the concept of creativity, new ideas and innovations in the minds and hearts of the children right from Sunday school to primary school education. We should create an ambience for the pursuit of alternative ideas and imaginations. The leaders/teachers in the church and institutions should be convinced of its significance and promising vision. Only then, there can be results and these results can be seen in a period of 10-15 years.

2. **Young students:** The church has avenues in introducing these concepts in a systematic way in youth groups/classrooms in the schools. They should be provided with opportunities to new thinking which results in creativity and innovation through small projects. Every opportunity must be created involving new ideas; to quote Dr. Abdul Kalam, 'Dream, Dream and Dream', as we engage, these bold dreams should become our propelling point. Opportunities should be created, and spaces should be provided to the young minds to share their ideas through social media and other school related opportunities.

3. **Adults:** Colleges and institutions of higher learning have much greater opportunity to convert the learned concepts into actions.

Their energy and enthusiasm can be synergized to collectively analyze their learnings and thus, leading to meaningful actions. Young people appreciate new ideas and are open for change and innovation. Church leaders and teachers should never snub any new ides emerging from them. We should always encourage youth to experiment new ideas so that real education can be visualized.

Conclusion

The ideas that are expressed in this article mainly entails the concept of creativity, innovation and imagination, and the need to nurture these among the children, young minds and adults as part of the Education ministry of the Church. Church is disciplined and ordained to remain inclusive. As Christians, we are called to possess the humility to subscribe all that we have achieved to the Gracious Hand of God; for God is the one who enables us to receive such blessings just like the witness of Nehemiah (Nehemiah 2:10). With the same kind of humility, Daniel acknowledged God for the knowledge and wisdom he received from God. Therefore, my dear friends, as we deliberate and plan many things, let us not forget that education is a creative gift that God has given to us to be shared with all men and women for fostering creativity, free thinking and innovation.

2

Education: Transforming the Margins

S. Angelin Sheeja

Education is the gateway to the global integrated framework of sustainable development goals. It is the third eye of a person to enrich our knowledge and wisdom to develop our ideas and concept. It helps to explore our own thoughts and ideas and makes it able to share it to others. It is the door to our destiny. Education is a process of facilitating learning or the acquisition of knowledge, skills, values, beliefs, and habits. Educational methods include storytelling, discussion, teaching, training and directed research. The educator adopts the methodology of teaching which is called pedagogy.

Etymologically, the term education is derived from the Latin word, *ēdūcō* which means 'I lead forth', 'I take out', 'I raise up', 'I erect' or 'draw out'. In Latin, *educare* means to lead away from the darkness of ignorance to the light of wisdom. Historically speaking, storytelling passed knowledge, values, and skills from one generation to the next. Adults trained the young with the knowledge and skills necessary in their society. To be specific, education is the being and becoming of an individual. It aims to bring out the inner strengths and helps to focus on the areas of strength for the overall development.

The need for discussion on the purpose of education in the 21st century is rooted in sustaining and enhancing the dignity, capacity, and welfare of the human person in relation to other and to nature. The age, in which we live, is characterized by alteration, entanglement and contradiction. In such a scenario, a humanistic approach in education reaffirms the universal set patterns. It promotes the acquisition of relevant knowledge and the development of competencies in the service of our common humanity. It has a central concern for inclusiveness and for an education that does not exclude and marginalize.

The humanistic values that should be the foundation and purpose of education include respect for life and human dignity, equal rights and social justice, cultural and social diversity, a sense of human solidarity and shared responsibility for our common future. By following such principles, we can reject learning systems that alienate individuals, that treat them like commodities, and of social practices that divide and dehumanize people. Education can be the transformative and empowering force to achieve sustainability and peace. It becomes the concern for global development. Education with new ideas and ideals addresses multiple dimensions like social, ethical, economic, cultural, civic, and spiritual.

The 1996 Delors' Report has produced four pillars of learning. They are:

- **Learning to Know** - A broad general knowledge, a depth on small number of subjects.

- **Learning to Do** - To acquire occupational skills in addition to the competence to deal with many situations and work in teams.

- **Learning to Be** - To develop one's personality and to be able to act with growing autonomy, judgment and personal responsibility.

- **Learning to Live Together** - By developing an understanding of other people and an appreciation for inter-dependence.

Education must go beyond the social and cultural dimensions of human interaction in concern for the relationship of human society with the natural environment. Our human history has witnessed blots of discretion and seclusion over the years. The redrawing of border during the fall on Constantinople, the Roman capital had allowed the learned literates to cross borders and that had affected on the amalgamation of the movement. During Renaissance, the spirit of inquiry was instilled in the human minds through education. It brought about drastic changes in social, political, and religious arena. Especially in religion, October 31, 1517 CE is marked as the Protestant Reformation which had its beginning with Martin Luther nailing 95 Theses on the walls of Wittenberg Cathedral, Germany. The Church took heed to focus on Revival, Renewal, and Restoration by pointing out the congregation to repent, return, and reform.

As we are commemorating 500 years of Reformation and the 70th year of Church of South India, the need of the hour is to create a borderless community in Christianity by transcending the borders. God's oneness has taught us to be united to each other. As said in the Lord's Prayer (John 17:22), oneness and unity is the core message of Jesus Christ. In today's rapidly changing world, the transformative force that heightens the purpose of education should promote human rights and dignity, to eradicate poverty and deepen sustainability, to build a better future for all, founded on equal rights and social justice, respect for cultural diversity and international solidarity and shared responsibility. These are the fundamental aspects of our common humanity as suggested by Director General of UNESCO, Irina Bokova.

Today, the idea of education dwells in the world of consumerism. This understanding is in contrary to what the Bible teaches. Isaiah 1:17 says, *'Learn to do well; seek judgement, relieve the oppressed, judge the fatherless, plead for the widow'.* Jesus stood to the advocacy of the marginalized and remained a transformational counselor to all those who tried to transform the margins. Evidences are found in the gospels.

A few are highlighted below:

1. Jesus sent his disciples away to do the mission (Luke 9:1,2, 10:1,2). The disciples spread away and crossed the borders to form borderless community of understanding and faith.

2. Jesus challenged the oppressive communities (Luke 19:41,42). Jesus was heart-broken over the rebellious nature of Jerusalem's inhabitants. Jesus wept over the communities and calls to love one another. Jesus faced struggles and humiliation when he challenged the dehumanizing law codes.

3. Jesus embraced other cultures (John 4). Jesus embodied a cross-cultural gospel focus. He was not afraid or was offended by the Samaritans. The heart of Jesus is for people. It is well-illustrated in the life-changing conversation Jesus had with a woman at a well. The Holy Spirit has established the church in a multicultural, multilingual environment (Act 1:8). We are commissioned to reach out to every culture and people group on earth.

4. Jesus surrounded himself with the lost people (Luke 15:1). Tax collectors and sinners listened to him. He was kind to the adulterous woman (John 8:1-11) and Zacchaeus the tax collector (Luke 19:11). By offering grace and truth, the lost were drawn to him to be transformed. The most beautiful element of our church is people enjoy a transforming relationship with Jesus Christ. The missionaries from several parts of the world communed with our ancestors who were then living in the clutches of slavery and caste discrimination. They took initiatives to relieve them from such dungeon and

led them towards transformation.

5.   Jesus recognized the needs of the people (John 11:35). Jesus wept for the death of Lazarus. He was a man who deeply loved others. He felt their pain. Jesus was compassionate towards the 'weary and worn out, (who were) like sheep without a shepherd' (Mat 9:35-37). Jesus cared for people who were hungry and meek. He cared for the physically sick and the spiritually oppressed.

6.   Jesus was eco-friendly (Matthew 5). In this passage, we Jesus being attached to the people who were associated with soil, sand and water. From the margins to the synagogue, he transformed his pedagogy towards the hills, mountains and seas. It altered the marginalized by pulling them towards nature. Nature educates them life and reality. According to C. S. Lewis, a Christian apologist, 'the task of the modern educator is not to cut down jungles but to irrigate deserts'. Such transformation would empower the margins to explore new paths.

Conclusion

Jesus came to educate and serve the community which was marginalized. In him, we witness the greatest transformation of the margins, the world has ever known. Jesus led out of his character and heart for the world to transform the margins. As educators, we are called to reflect Jesus Christ. On the 23rd of February, in Kerala, Madhu, 27-year young tribal was apprehended by a mob that accused him of the theft and was beaten to death. This news shook the state. The Chief Minister retorted saying, 'A civilized society cannot tolerate such heinous act'. Even horrific did it turned when a man was found taking selfie with the injured victim and the picture went viral. Where is humanity heading to?

Modern inventions have crushed our humanity within. If Kerala, the state which tops in literacy rate, could witness to such a horrendous act, it is high time, we turn our attention to the kind of education that our society adheres to. Let us turn to Jesus and follow his footsteps; to focus on the marginalized and the downtrodden is the call of the Church. It would widen the angle to foster learning through life. Let us continue to respond to the needs of the communities through the formation of educational partnership.

3

Rethinking Ecclesia- Empowerment and Education Perspective:

Rethinking Christian Education in today's Context: Towards a Borderless Church.

"Theory divides and Praxis unites."

Krupa Victor

Thank you for the invitation to participate and to contribute to this important conference on Rethinking-Ecclesia-Empowerment and Education Perspective in connection with remembering the event of reformation. Reformation is an outcome of strategic collision of Faith, Christian Education and Education. Education played a decisive role in whole process of reformation.

1. Introduction: Contextual Challenges

The world is changing- education must also change. Societies everywhere are undergoing deep transformation, and this calls for new forms of education to foster the competencies that it creates both in secular and sacred realms. The complexity of our country with its diversities and differences of religion, caste, culture, language, people, geography, climate, politics, and economics, abilities and disabilities has been aggravated by economic liberalization, propelled by globalization and environmental degradation and people's struggle and quest for identity.

We notice the random technological development, global marketing and heavy usage of multi-media and communication technologies. Corruption, violence, terrorist attacks, indiscriminating shootings and mass killings, and communal riots, bomb blasts, discrimination based on caste, gender, class and violence against women, children, denial of justice and human rights, commercialization, consumerism, rise of religious fundamentalism and fanaticism, degradation of moral and ethical values and lack of appropriate role models to emulate continue to exist in the church and society. Hence, progress and massive poverty, inequality based on gender, caste, class, violence, injustice and exclusion at all levels of human life have become philosophy of life. The church is also influenced and affected by all these complexities, processes in its life and ministry in the context. In such a context Christian faith continues to be challenged by the forces. Christians are called to live out faith in a world of changes and strive to establish the Kingdom of God, where borders are crossed over in order to experience the wellbeing in life on earth.

This paper is an attempt to reflect on the theme, Rethinking Christian Education in the Present Context: Towards a Borderless Church by revisiting the understanding of "Christian Education activity, approaches and its role in the life and ministry of the church. How do we define Christian Education?

2.   Christian Education: Defined

Education as process contributes to build some boundaries and also removes some borders. Christian Education is an integral part of Christian ministry and the back bone of the ministry of nurturing in Christian faith. As such it is grounded in the divine involvement in the world. The focus of Christian Ministry is to enable and empower the members of the Christian community to find the ways of putting their innate potentialities at the disposal of God's work in the world. Therefore, Christian Ministry first and foremost is an activity of liberation. It is by participating in God's activities we appropriate our being humans and experience the liberation that God offers to us. It demands an effort of being conscious, alert and attentive to God's praxis in both sacred and secular spheres or in the Church and the world. Christian Ministry cannot be limited to the ministry of and to the Christian community only and it is open to all and it requires an intentionality to facilitate discernment of and dedication to God's praxis in the world. Therefore, Christian Education is understood as the intentional and systematic teaching ministry of the Church, which aims to meet the needs of all age groups in the congregations. In other words, Christian Education is a religious undertaking rooted in Christian faith, and it is the means, through which God in Christ carry on His redemptive work in the day to day life experiences of an individual.

In other words, Christian Education is an attempt to make available for our generation- children, young people and adults- the accumulated treasures of Christian life and thought, in such a way that God, in Christ may carry on His redemptive work in each human soul and in the common life of (man) human beings.[1] The aim of Christian education is both transmission of tradition as well as social and personal transformation, which alerts and enables one to be in partnership in God's redemptive activity in this world.

As an agent of God's redemptive activity, the focus of Christian Ministry through its educational ministry is to enable, facilitate and empower the members of Christian community, so that the members are made ***conscious, alert and attentive to God's praxis*** not only in the Church but also in the world. It is integrally related to God's liberating activity in the world.[2] Hence, Christian Education is an intentional activity of facilitating discernment of and dedication to God's praxis in the world, which is a dynamic process of formation and transformation of all aspects of human life.[3] It provides an opportunity to the church to play a prophetic role; Christian Education is a prophetic activity in its context.

So Christian Education can be defined as an intentional Educational process is to "awaken" "alert" and "deepen" one's faith.[4] It is a deliberate attempt to promote lived Christian faith hence it is a prophetic ministry and by playing a prophetic role it seeks to transform people, structures and society. Therefore, Christian Education is an activity of transcending the borders in continuation of the Jesus' Ministry that was entrusted to disciples and the apostles. It is a ministry of enabling people to realize and experience the Kingdom of God on earth.

3.   Mission Education Past and Present: Empowerment or Enslavement?

Christian education programs are crucial for Christian nurture and provide platform and occasion for teaching ministry. During the missionary era education was given priority and through schools, hostels, and other church related institutions Christian nurture took place. Mission pillars are education, hospital and church/ congregation, which were very vibrant in crossing borders of religion, caste, class, gender and other borders that divided and excluded people from each others to certain extent. Mission through its educational ministry has attempted to bring awareness of social evils, eradicate poverty and social discrimination, stigma, empowered people at the margins to gain human dignity, identity and social status. It was both strategic collision of Gospel, faith and education, thus was able to transcend borders to enable people to experience the love of God in action.

In the present context, faith education or teaching is mostly imparted through the agencies such as Sunday school, VBS,

Confirmation Classes, Youth fellowship, Women's Fellowship, Cottage Prayer Meeting besides regular Worship and Preaching and other occasions and meetings based on the events and so on. Apart from these normal and regular programs, there are fellowship meetings, family enriching programs and other teaching and learning activities organized at different contexts. These are the initial contexts where Christian Education is carried in most of the churches and normally attended by different age groups in the church or the congregation. In rural areas the Sunday school is the only place where Christian education is imparted for whole congregation irrespective of their age group.

In the urban Churches, often the formal Christian education is imparted with the help of Christian education curriculum that are available. However, a critical evaluation of the content of the syllabus used shows that it neither connects to the hearts of the teachers or the children, nor to the world in which these children are to grow and other members to grapple with. The possible reason for this could be lack of commendable level of readiness brought by this teaching to equip them to face the world as a Christian and citizen. In terms of methodologies often there is no effort to look at the most contemporary methods and research in teaching and possibilities to leave an impact on the minds of the children. Often the need of relating the message of the Bible stories to the life experiences of the learners in the Indian context is ignored and totally neglects their emotions and feelings and capabilities to be creative thinkers. The teachers quiet often perceive their task as leading the child to accept Jesus Christ as the primary task of Christian education. This kind of individualistic and other worldly approach to Christian Education continues to hamper our educational ministry in present context.

The present generation is a learning generation. Connected and inter-connected to various avenues of teaching and learning processes. The church has a tremendous task and opportunity to connect through the right kind of media and cater to through effective methods of teaching. The interconnectedness of the people in the corporate body has to enhance the harmony of worship. The right use of media will enrich and provide possibility to be connected with and foster inter-connectedness of the congregation through the teaching ministry in the church. There should also other avenues to foster enrichment programs, gender awareness, career guidance; women empower programs, self-help groups, managing finances, identity affirmation-awareness to their rights as members in minority status in the state and country, marriage and pre-marital counseling and others can become resorts which can be turned as educating contexts. As such, Christian education activities continue to maintain the status quo rather than becoming an agency of transformation.

Education Liberates and it's is liberation and empowerment. Education as practice of freedom is to be discerned as leaping beyond borders in order to become Christ communities. Paulo Freire, the Brazilian educator, proponent of a critical and radical pedagogy – pedagogy of the oppressed has discerned education as dynamic and transformative. It is not neutral but biased- biased to be both being and becoming.

According to Richards Shaull, "there is no such thing as neutral education process. Education either functions as an instrument which is used to facilitate the integration of the younger generation into the logic of the present system and bring about conformity to it, or it becomes the practice of freedom,"[5] the means by which men and women deal critically and creatively with reality and discover how to participate in the transformation of their world. Education and empowerment are the pillars of the mission of the church in India. Education played and must continue to play a vital role in setting the direction for the church and the society *to be and to become.* As such, Christian Education has to become the means and the agency of actualizing that vision of being and becoming. What are those possibilities that can assist Christian Education in the present context to become an agency of being and becoming-in order to become borderless church?

4.   Re-Thinking Christian Education: Towards a Borderless Church

a.   *Christian Education is an ongoing process of equipping people of God*

Christian education cannot become a finished product but it is an ongoing process of learning, re-learning and un-learning activity. It is an activity of faith formation and transformation moves forward not stagnant. This unfinished character of education and the transformational character of reality necessitates that education be an ongoing activity. Education is thus constantly remade in the praxis, in order to be, it must become. As such it not only takes impetus from the contextual issues, but it also contributes to the educational formulations. The primary goal and objective of such ongoing educational activity is redemption of human beings and liberation from the oppressive structures and systems that perpetuate oppression, exclusion in order to transcend the borders that are created and emerged from time to time. In short, it is joining hands with the creative and redemptive act of God to do away with the disparity, exclusion to be inclusive and open to the changes. Therefore, education is not just "knowing" but it is also "becoming, it is praxis oriented" aimed at not only for change of individual persons but also for change of oppressive structures and systems in the church and society. Christian Education as an ongoing process needs to provide the means and ways to make the members to be aware of and attentive to the changes in the context. Hence, equipping, empowering and to edifying becomes a crucial task. To equip members through its educational ministry the churches must have a well prepared curriculum or a syllabi which provides a room for the learners to examine and re-examine their faith appropriation in the day to day context. Equipping the local congregations needs to be given much importance. Organizing learning programs to strengthen the laity in order to inculcate and provide role model to be emulated is the need of the hour. The changed context always stimulates rethinking of the past, what happened before them lies open to numerous possible understandings. The past is always open-never finished".[6]

Traditional Christian Religious Education negates the fuller human life by propagating exclusive form of the culture of the context,[7] and fails to relate the liberative message of the Gospel to the daily life situations of the people. Therefore, Christian education in the present context must attempt to interpret God's liberative power in the light of the real life situations and/or existential realities of the people, by employing the hermeneutical task of re-reading the Bible in one's own context, thereby motivating them move towards experiencing the liberative transformation in their lives.

The, "the Prophetic Church, like Christ, must move forward constantly, forever dying and being reborn. In order to be, it must always be in a state of becoming. The prophetic Church must also accept an existence which is in dramatic tension between past and future, staying and going, speaking the word and keeping silence, being and not being. There is no prophecy without risk. Thus Christian Education is an instrument of transforming and transcending action on move. It is a political praxis at the service of permanent human liberation. This does not happen only in the consciousness of people but, presupposes a radical change of structures in which the process of consciousness will itself be transformed."[8]

b. *Christian Education is to be perceived as Ecumenical Education*

The Church is God's gift to the community. As such it has a unique privilege to involve itself along with God as "Co-worker" in God's liberative activity going beyond borders by taking risk. Re-reading the Bible in terms of our context is not enough unless it leads into a critical awareness and Christian praxis of shaping reality in the faith journey. Christian Education as Ecumenical Education seeks to attempt and foster understanding of, commitment to and informed participation in the Ecumenical Process through its educational ministries and its main agenda is to promote justice, peace, tolerance and common good of all. The term 'ecumenism' is understood as 'church unity' but this term 'Ecumenical' can never be limited to the history of attempts to unity of churches or the growth of ecumenical organizations.

Ecumenical Education means moving towards holistic spirituality provides with the tools of critical consciousness to see how reality is being detained to be empowered and to act for social transformation in line with the prophetic witness of the gospel.[9] This proposal to make Christian education activity as ecumenical education emphasises the importance of the human community which is in interaction and integration with the community of the church. Often Christian Educational activity is understood by the Churches as maintaining status quo rather than work for the conscientization of the people. Hence seeks legitimize perpetual discrimination and prejudice against each others in the Church based on their caste and/or class/gender identity. Instead, Christian Education must help not just to nurture the faith of the learners, but it must also prepare individuals for real life by including in its educational agenda the issues such as 'cultural nationalism', 'multi-faith context' and 'ecological concerns', other social concerns and struggle for 'human dignity and solidarity' and other contextual issues.[10]

Hence, ecumenical learning and learning methods of dialogue is an essential tool to move forward to experience and enable others to experience togetherness in community as one body. The teacher-learner relation is collegial attempting together to building human community based on justice, peace and love. Christian Education needs to include this missing dimension of ecumenical perspective in order to prepare generations to live meaningfully, creatively and humanely together by transcending all disparities. This living together is for living for one another (Koinonia), all peoples and all faiths learning, where every one finds themselves belonged to and accepted.

Engaging in dialogue, conversation and encounter between and among seekers, finders, and keepers of faith becomes the main agenda. This gives the scope to incorporate the non biblical content in its educational activity. The core of the problem that Religious Education in India faces is "the reconciliation of the two aspects of the dichotomized understanding of Christian faith and life in the world in a discerning manner."[11] So the task of Christian Education is to discern a holistic approach of life that affirms human dignity by giving room to challenge and enable people to go beyond the brokenness of human situation to build deeper sustained and sustaining relationships which is foundational to our faith pilgrimage. Ecumenical Education takes place in the creative manner with the co-operation of communities of different faiths, traditions, and cultures. This provides a possibility to inculcate transformed human values, bring attitudinal changes and in turn it will become a catalyst in transforming the whole creation. Thus the Church has a very unique role to play and commit itself for the ministry of transformation.

c. *Christian Education has to become a Life-Affirming Activity*

Life affirmation always implies resist, confront and eliminate all that negates life. An essential character of liberation is affirmation of life and inter-relatedness. The fullness of life can be realized only within the web of inter-relationship of all beings. It means a relationship that relates everything not as rulers or masters, but as co-workers and co-pilgrims in faith journey.[12] Hence , Christian Education is life centred activity aims at preparing people in all contexts to opt for life and be in solidarity with those, whose life is threatened, marginalized, and oppressed, all who struggle for their liberation, through working towards creating a New Humanity in Christ.

Christian Education Activity is to be perceived as a harmony in diversity.   Diversity is God's structure of creation, God works in diversity. Diversity expresses God's richness.[13] No culture and no community are excluded from God's structure of creation. All are unique in their own way. Therefore, no one has right to dominate, discriminate, exclude and suppress others. Life is to be protected and it can grow to its fullness only by the affirmation of the beauty of diversity and life. Because to live a life of inter-connectedness is cosmic design of God and affirmation of life and human dignity is the basis of liberation.

Christian Education as life centred activity is concerned with the management of life, stewardship of life, sharing and cultivating of life, safeguarding and producing justice and celebration of life. It implies a shift from content-oriented cognitive knowledge and individualistic education activity into an educational process that affirms life. It enables to equip people to face the realities of life. Acquiring knowledge to promote life, rediscover and re-affirm the life of the dehumanized on the earth is the original scope and meaning of *Oikumene*; it is concerned with the management of God's household. It challenges us to learn and inculcate a new spirituality of caring for each other by affirming life of the oppressor and oppressed.[14] There can be no separation between human and culture, no conflict between culture and nature. The Church through its educational ministry must work in collaboration with likeminded people, agencies and nongovernmental organizations and promote social justice and liberation. Church should stand by the people who struggle to gain human rights and thus envision establishing the Kingdom of God here and now.

Let us, as churches enter into an act of covenanting, and commit ourselves to fight against all evils both in the church and society to build a just community and build co-operation between communities and religions and work towards establishment of justice, peace and the integrity of creation in our context.[15]

d. Christian Education is an activity of working with the People and not for the People

People are not mere spectators but actual participants in the ministry and mission of God in and through the Church. This shift in emphasis is to be found its due place in the process of Christian Education. Christian Education is a ministry; carried out in the midst of cultural, social and religious diversities This is so because God never used people to advocate on their behalf but God came down to be in solidarity and radical engagement in the context, with the oppressed against the oppressors. This changed understanding and faith appropriation challenges the whole activity of Christian Religious Education. Luke 4: 18-21 Jesus declaring the Manifesto, Jesus' manifesto of mission has direct implications for advocacy approach. It involves commitment to the cause. Advocacy approach is generally used on behalf of the oppressed, aiming at working against the structures and systems that continue to violate human rights.

This approach indeed has tremendous impact and it continues to play a positive role in raising the conscience of the oppressed groups such as women, dalits and tribals, children, violated, discriminated and marginalised groups of people to bring liberation.

Christian Education as the ministry of reconciliation, liberative and life affirmative activity (1 Corinthians 4: 21) has to reorient itself with an alternative approach of being in solidarity. It is a very powerful and prophetic agency of transformation of the structures. Solidarity is a Christian virtue; it is to be understood as human response to God and God's liberative mission on the earth. Being in solidarity is an expression of faith in God through participation. Hence, it is participatory solidarity and transformation which is in effect. It is standing on equal foot, standing together shoulder to shoulder along with victims, whoever it might be. It aims at fighting together for a world in which it will be possible for all sorts of victims to find a space to grow into fullness of life.[16]

In educational context, this approach seems an essential approach to be followed. By being in solidarity one enters into the situation of those with whom one is identifying and it is a radical posture. True solidarity with the oppressed is to fight at their side to transform the objective reality which has made the oppressed- 'beings for another'. A true solidarity is found only in the plenitude of act of love, in its existentiality. In this sense both the objectivity and the subjectivity are in constant dialectical relationship. Therefore, solidarity is both an action and human response to God's activity in the world.

Creation of a just society, envisioning borderless church is integral vision of Liberative Education, translation of this vision into reality is essential task and very crucial for Church's ministry. The translation of this vision into a reality is not an easy task. This becomes impossible as long as Church through its mission and ministry continues to work for God's people and play the role of advocacy only. Instead the Church through its Educational Ministry ought to work not only with them-the oppressed and the excluded but need to spread out in the society or in the world and work towards the transformation of all. This requires the Church to go through the experience of being revolutionary by passing over into the world of people.[17] It implies the necessity for a complete change from the previous position or status, going through the experience of "being buried" of all that oppresses others as well as the individuals- the oppressors. It means a complete transformation of the 'human being'- a new birthing experience because the ultimate vision of the Christian Education is creation of a just society.[18]

Translation of this vision into reality needs to focus on the question of how to work in the world. This brings the importance of Educational ministry of the Church if it wants to be an agency of liberation and transformation. To be able to become an agency of God's liberative transformation, the Educational ministry of the Churches in the context is to be freed from the layers of blinders, excluders, boundary markers and prejudices against people with different identity and orientation.

To be in participatory solidarity, Christian Education has to become an education with people but not for the people. The possible signpost found in the incarnation act of God in Jesus Christ. Incarnation of Christ in the world is the climax of God's solidarity with human beings. Being in solidarity or understanding Christian Education as a transformative activity with the people enables the Churches to become relevant to the Context because it is life centered and life affirming, its focus is preparing individuals to opt for life and to be in solidarity with all whose life is threatened. It requires 'Critical consciousnesses'. The unique purpose of Christian Education is to lead people to experience liberation in Christ. It is the Church alone can offer a hope of emancipation, because the Church has the mandate from Jesus Christ Himself to liberate. The Church must take up the Cross, to liberate and be in solidarity with. Solidarity has to be sustained whether Christians or not, the aspect of togetherness in solidarity is constructed against the forces which seek to legitimize their victimization and disrupt their communal life. Such sense of solidarity against dehumanization becomes a great source of strength for the Church to work towards empowering in a praxiological manner by seeking to re-integrate dehumanized into community disrupting status quo. This is possible only if the Church perceives its educational ministry as working with the people and not for the people. The church needs to integrate its ministries with organizations which work with people in seeking justice, human trafficking, bonded laborers and commercial sex workers and all marginal groups of people. Hence, the urgent need is to integrate them with the church, instead of treating as objects of charity, people to be thoughtful or prayed for.

Conclusion

In conclusion Christian Education activity invites us to enter into the world with the power of the Gospel to become the leaven, acquiring an outgoing character, leaven like thrust which means understanding ministry as *an activity centered in the Kingdom of God.* It seeks to take into account the enriching new factors that have come into light. It is essential because the changing phenomenon such as global outlook on reality, the multi religious character of the world, the cultural revival among people, and the growth and progress in scientific and technological fields, all these call for a new understanding of a Kingdom-Centered ministry for the modern world where the church becomes open without borders to embrace whole of God's creation.

Endnotes

[1] Randolph Crump Miller, *Education for Christian Living,* Englewood Cliffs: Prentice-Hall Inc., 1956, p. 54

[2] Mary Elizabeth Moore, *Education for Continuity and Change* (Nashvelli: Abingdon Press, 1983), 60-61.

[3] Samson Prabhakar, Essays on Christian Education and Liturgy, Bangalore: SATHRI/BTESSC, 2003 p. 83.

[4] James J. Deboy, Jr., Getting Started in Adult Religious Education: A Practical Guide, New York: Paulist Press, 1979, p. 55.

[5] Paulo Friere, *Pedagogy of the Oppressed,* Translated by M. B. Romos (New York: Heder & Heder, 1971), p. 4.

[6] Mary C. Boys, *Educating in Faith* (San Francisco: Harper and Row Publishers, 1989), 45.

[7] Samson Prabhakar, "Towards an Indian Christian Religious Education" (1990).

[8] Paulo Freire, "Education, Liberation, and the Church" in *Religious Education Journal,* Vol. 70, no. 4, Fall (1984): 542-548.

[9] Samson Prabhakar, "Towards a Religious Education for an Inclusive Community," *Bangalore Theological Forum* XXVIII, no. 3&4 (1996): 39.

[10] K. Rajaratnam, "Presidential Address," in *Christian Education in a Multi-Faith Society*, ed. Arun Gopal (Madras: CSI Synod, 1996), 6-7.

[11] Prabhakar, "Towards a Religious Education for an Inclusive Community," 85.

[12] Prabhakar, *Essays on Christian Education and Liturgy*, 56.

[13] Prabhakar, *Essays on Christian Education and liturgy.* p. 101.

[14] Conrad Raiser, "On the Eve of the Third Millennium," *NCC Review* CXXII, no. 4 (2000): 646.

[15] K. C. Abraham, *Liberative Solidarity: Contemporary Perspectives in Mission* (Tiruvalla: Christava Sahitya Samithi, 1996), 126.

[16] Massey, "Paradigm Shift in Theological Education: Advocacy to Solidarity," 17-18.

[17] Paulo Freire & Antonio Faundez, *Learning to Question, a Pedagogy of Liberation* (Geneva: WCC Publications, 1989), 54-56.

[18] Stanley Aronowitz, "Paulo Freire's Radical Democratic Humanism," in *Paulo Freire a Critical Encounter*, ed. Peter McLaren and Peter Leonard (New York/London: Routledge 1993), 235.

4

Education: Transforming the Margins

Kamala Dhawale

We would all readily agree that education is a life changing, life enhancing and not to forget, a life-long process; a process that has transformed lives and changed situations; a process that has been a catalyst for not only transformations but also an initiator for revolutions and ground- breaking changes. History bears proof that once the importance of education was established, a systematic way of imparting it was evolved over a period of time. However, it should not be denied that in the past, education was relegated only to the elite. It was only after the middle ages, during Renaissance and Reformation that the voice of Martin Luther was heard above that of other reformers to bring about a change in the mode of education which had thus far found shelter in the monasteries.

In his open letter to the Christian nobility, Martin Luther wrote, *"I believe that there is no work more worthy of pope or emperor than a thorough reform of the universities"*. Others who were enlightened joined Martin Luther in universalizing education with the main intent of creating an enlightened society. With this early attempt of liberalising education, Martin Luther paved the way for education being one major area where Church could minister. Since then, the Church has valued each human being as equal, and has placed education on its top priority list. A glance at the major universities worldwide would show us that they were founded, funded and flourished as ministries of the Church.

It was the Church and the Missionaries who reached out to the society with the education ministry. The two other fields that the Church prioritised, besides spreading the word of God, were education and medicine. Nonetheless, these two important fields were largely neglected and ignored when it came to the marginalised. Times were such that people could not think beyond hard work and eking out a decent living. Times were hard and conditions were extremely harsh. The lives of the marginalized were so pathetic that even getting a decent meal per day was a struggle. Education was way beyond their reach and ken.

To add to the woes, the social structure was such that education was the treasured possession of the upper class. The duty of the lower class was to do the bidding of their masters. Education was a guarded treasure, held closed and confined by and to the higher-class society. The thought of education for all, education as a basic right of an individual was not only a distant dream, but also an impossibility.

When the missionaries came to India, the divide between the educated and the uneducated was immense. The upper class, though highly educated, spared no effort but kept the lower class of the society ignorant, slavish and forever looking up to them. Among the first things that the missionaries did was to learn the language of the locals. When they witnessed the situation, they realised that the best way to elevate the pathetic condition of the down trodden and the marginalised was through education. The tenet 'Christ is for all' drove the missionaries to do their best and to bring the marginalised to the centre. The desire to reach out to the neglected and the ignored, the rejected and the marginalised consumed them like fire. The main intent of the Church was to embrace all in its fold, help them stand on their own, give them the confidence and dignity they never had. The missionaries believed that the education was the only means of bridging the gap. Inclusiveness became the key word.

The Church took upon itself the mammoth task of bringing education to the lowly masses. One is left to imagine the wrath of the upper class when the Church had taken on this task. The road was long and arduous. The Church set out to establish schools where they were none. The main concern of the Church was to reach out to the marginalised. The marginalised did not mean just the lower strata of the society but it also included the poor, the neglected and most importantly the women. Schools were established, some exclusively for the girls. Education had to start literally from the scratch. New paths had to be paved, new courses chartered.

The situation was grim. There were no text books as such. The missionaries wrote the text books. No school building existed for the marginalized, so they built them. The Church played a major role in public education. The slow trickle of students soon became a deluge. More and more children from the marginalised sections were coming to schools. Raising funds became a herculean task. The children of the poor masses could hardly afford the fees. The Church had not only to construct school buildings, maintain the infrastructure, pay the teachers, but also manage everything on a shoe string budget. Education was made available to the masses. With the floodgates of education open, people sent their children to school and made the best use of the facility that till now was an unreachable dream for them. The Church advocated borderless society, which they felt could be attained only through education.

Missionaries, especially Rev. Dr. Ferdinand Kittel, took education one step further. Besides writing text books and formulating a syllabus, he wrote books on Kannada grammar. The pioneering work in the field of Kannada language and literature was undertaken by Rev. Kittel. Most importantly, he gave Kannada the Kannada-English Dictionary, a stellar work that none has surpassed till date. His contribution has enriched the Kannada language and literature. Rev. Dr. Kittel was one of the many missionaries who worked tirelessly to educate the poor and the marginalised. With the selfless efforts of the Church and the missionaries, as Rev. Kittel envisioned, education and the love of education spread; within a span of a few decades, people were made aware of many things and of the world around that were to them hitherto unknown.

Education transformed their lives. Knowledge opened their eyes to their rights and individual freedom. Education broadened their horizon. The freedom that education brought further enhanced their social, cultural, economic and spiritual life. It was the breath of fresh, cleansing air that brought life and light to the almost dead souls. The Church provided them with what they needed. As the Chinese proverb goes, 'A journey of a thousand miles begins with a single step', the walk had begun. The Church saw the establishment of the primary school, then the secondary and the journey continues. The Church in its effort to reach out to the marginalised established the major stake in higher education scenario in our country.

The legacy continues; our schools and colleges still cater to the less privileged and the have nots. Our educational institutions are doing much to elevate their position and draw the marginalised to be included in the society. These students are from all faiths and benefits are provided alike. Many such students who have imbibed discipline, values and Christian principles bear witness in places where they are employed. Many successful individuals, who hold and have held prominent positions in the society remember with fondness the prayers that they learnt at school along with moral values, ethics and

Christian principles which have helped them reach greater heights. However, with the passage of time, the table seemed to have turned. A big question stares at the Church today. Have we in our efforts, to transform the marginalised, ended up being the marginalised?

A sea change has occurred in the field of education now. The Church, the initiator of education, has in the present scenario been relegated to the fringe. In today's world, where education has been commercialised, the Church, which has always looked to education as a service, has been left way behind in the race. The educational institutions started by the Church are at a risk, fighting for survival and space in this new sprung cut-throat educational climate. Funding is at risk if government guidelines are not complied with. With the constant changing of Educational policies of the government and the new educational institutions with their state of infrastructure and equipment, exorbitant donations and flashy advertisements, the question remains. The challenge before us today is - Where do we stand? How can we compete?

All is not lost. It is not impossible to reinvigorate the role of the Church in education. Can we not reclaim education as something that the Church provides? We have reached a time where, the Christian community, in whatever sphere of work we are placed, should initiate efforts and actions to look at our schools and colleges as mission fields, just like what our missionaries did. A lot would change if we who are working in educational institutions see our work not as a job, as means of livelihood but as a ministry and the other members can continue to pray for the institutions, the teachers and the students. The Church can once again closely associate with the institutions and find out what their needs are and have regular prayer cells in the institutions. This is lacking in many of our institutions today. Earlier every institution used to set aside a day where the teachers got together and spent time in Bible study and prayer. However, this practice has lost its significance with the change of contexts and the evolving trends.

Government has provided various schemes for the benefit of the marginalised. How could the marginalized be identified? How can the Church help them? All said and done, there are sections of people who continue to live at the fringe of the society - We as a Church, as an educational institution, should reach out to families that are economically weak, families with health issues, where children cannot afford good education, families whose children have special needs, and most importantly single moms; there are women who are struggling to make ends meet and to provide a decent education for their kids; there are youths who are victims of substance abuse who are in need of counselling and rehabilitation; there are children who are infected with HIV patients and needs immediate medical care. Yes, the Church can transform their lives. And who is the Church? We are.

There are many retired teachers, administrators and academicians in our Churches who have the expertise and the time to bring about a transformation in the lives of the neglected teens, rejected youths and the school drop outs. There are many couples with empty nests who can support the church with their help. There are many economically well-off people who can afford to provide scholarships to the deserving and desirous students to finish a course.

The Church has to be strengthened to reach out to the marginalised. The gospel is for everyone. God created everyone in God's image. We are all equal. God's question to Cain was, 'Where is Abel, your brother?' (Genesis 4:9). This is applicable to all of us, even today. Jesus' ministry was one of love and compassion. He reached out to the marginalised. So, should we. Jesus' command 'love one another as I have loved you' (John 15:12) should reign supreme in all of us.

5

Knowledge Expansion and Border Crossing:

Lessons from the Life of a Missionary Teacher

Mini Chacko

The Higher education scenario today has gone borderless. Thanks to the two revolutions, namely globalization and Information technology, that has successfully narrowed down and erased the boundaries of time, space, geography and level. The ultimate gain of globalization is consumerism that runs the world today. Sitting at home, we can order for something we want from distant places like USA or Singapore. Similarly, we can take up a course from anywhere in the world. Consumerism has led us to amassing wealth and objects beyond our requirement and getting things at the snap of their fingers. This has pushed us towards a faster way of life, bringing along with-it intolerance in every walk of life.

Adversely, Information technology has shrunk the world to a small device called the cell phone, on which we can depend on, for anything and everything. About twenty years ago, when the cell phones were introduced, many of us resisted from using it, but today, we cannot do without it. We book tickets, pay bills, browse for recipes, clear doubts and expand our knowledge base. It has become a part of each one's existence today. Invariably, we have become so independent, that there is a great void in inter-personal relationships. Along with this, there is a decline in the values like truth, love, nonviolence, peace and right conduct. So, eventually, borders are being drawn within the present community likely– a generation divide, a digital divide and political communities with different ideologies. A seemingly trivial incident that causes anguish, is worth a mention here, to drive home the pros and cons of the present educational system.

> A mom asked her son who just came back from his Sunday school classes: Jimmy, what did you learn today?
>
> The son answered: Mom, we were taught about a leader called Moses, who took a great army, across a river on a bridge that he created – at the press of a remote button. And, after crossing it, before the enemy could climb the bridge, he pressed another button and destroyed the bridge.
>
> Mom aghast, asked Jimmy: Is that how they taught you?
>
> To which, Jimmy's answer was, "Mom, you wouldn't believe, if I tell you the way I was taught."

Jimmy represents today's generation and the incident clearly indicates his intolerance to the way he was being taught and the violence brewing in him. The need of the hour therefore, is an evolution of our community. The University Grants Commission has initiated this process by introducing Environmental science and Human Rights, as part of the UG Curriculum across all programs of study. Through this intervention, UGC envisions a community which is rich in ethical values. But nothing can be achieved without the teacher. Teachers are the ones who set the tone of their classrooms, build a warm environment, mentor and nurture students, listen to them and look for signs of trouble, expand the knowledge of students and become their role models.

Rev. Benjamin Bailey, the first missionary Principal of CMS College, Kottayam, Kerala, is a teacher worth emulating. It was his untiring efforts that transformed a small village of Kerala situated on the banks of Meenachil River into the present-day Kottayam. When Rev. Benjamin Bailey set foot in 1816, Kottayam fostered just three hundred inhabitants, verdant vegetation and a host of feudal values. As a few decades rolled by, it developed into a large town and transformed into the cultural and print media capital of Kerala. The onus for this goes to Rev. Bailey, the architect of present-day Kottayam, who functioned as the stimulus behind the College Kottayam, Printing press and the Holy Trinity CSI church that formed the nucleus, around which Kottayam town grew. Printing led to publishing books and periodicals. This popularized reading, and led Kerala, to universalization of public instruction, development of communication means and dissemination of knowledge. This in turn, culminated in social reforms, enlightenment and development of culture, eventually, pushing out the parochial feudal system unceremoniously. During his tenure as Principal from 1817-19, Rev. Bailey laid the foundation for modern education - modelled on Western Education. He formulated the curricula and syllabi and started teaching the English language. Thus, he became the founder of 'Modern liberal Education in Kerala. Rev. Bailey did not hesitate to cross the borders that limited him, when it came to transforming the Kottayam society.

A multifaceted personality, Rev. Bailey was the progenitor of printing and Book publishing in Malayalam, the native language of Kerala, first lexicographer in the language, first translator of the complete Bible into Malayalam and the first compiler of the Malayalam Dictionary. Besides, he was a well-versed author and translator. All of this helped him in knowledge expansion and dissemination. Rev. Bailey was not only an architect of letters, but also, an original architect in Gothic style. During the 1839-42 periods, he designed and built the beautiful Anglican Church in Kottayam – which Bishop Wilson called "The Glory of Travancore".

Rev. Benjamin Bailey, along with Rev. Henry Baker and Rev. Joseph Fenn, were called the "Kottayam Trio", the CMS missionaries who lived and worked together in harmony. Instead of limiting themselves to each one's area of activity, their borders overlapped when it came to sharing of resources. In 1818, Rev. Bailey focused his attention entirely on to translation and printing. He took upon himself the mission of translating the Bible into Malayalam, in a style that would be acceptable to the majority who had no education to speak of, as well as the minority, who were great scholars. Thus, he adopted the style – which he called "The middle path style", a blend of high and colloquial Malayalam, in prose style. Ironing out the creases and erasing the dividing lines within a community to balance it, makes Rev. Benjamin Bailey a role model for every teacher.

Rev. Bailey was the first among missionaries who came to Travancore at the invitation of the Colonel John Munroe in order to reform the ancient Syrian Christian Church and rid it of the superstitions that had crept into it. The missionaries were to love all, but, at the same time stand firm against practices that may lead to harm. All this said and done, it was only in 2010 that the Anglican Church accepted Darwin's Theory of Evolution. When asked, which theory should be taught in schools, the Church gave the green signal to teach both - the theory of Creation and the theory of Evolution, and let the students decide on how to integrate both, a giant step in knowledge expansion and border crossing.

6

Education:
Towards overcoming Creed, Caste and Class
V. Regina

Introduction

Children deserve the opportunity to succeed. But it is harder than ever to find a path out of poverty without a college education or technical training. Low-income students are six times more likely to drop out of high school and less than one third of them could enroll in college. A 6th grade student who misses over 20% of the class, whose teacher reports poor behaviour, or who fails Math or English is 70% more likely to drop out. While the state and the nation are trying to produce workers with skills to master new technologies and adapt to complexities of a global economy, school budgets have become tedious than ever. Summer learning loss is a primary cause of the persistent academic achievement gap.

The secular state is under constant threat. When we look at the global context and the crisis our secular state face, one can understand that the main challenge of the state is the emerging religious nationalism. Caste and class are opposites. In our present context, caste is replaced by class. Caste is a rural phenomenon whereas class is found in urban industrial settings. Caste is a closed system and does not permit immobility, whereas class is an open system and allows immobility for its members. Caste system is a construct where the society is divided up into several sets of contained and completely segregated units (*jatis*); the mutual relations between the units are ritually determined in a graded scale. Caste is a destructive system which pervades the whole of Hindu society in India and it is an encompassing system. Class in India has existed along with caste and power.

Our history unearths wicked and malicious brutality targeted against the Dalits, Tribals and the subalterns. We have attacked the Dalits and murdered a few; their women-folk were raped and put to indignities. Sinha observes that it is class war against Harijans and not atrocities. Ambedkar rightly observed that the caste system was not merely the division of labour, but also a division of laborers.

Education

Education in India has a long and complex history. The sheer variety of languages, peoples, cultures, geographical and climatic conditions required diverse approaches to impart knowledge and skills to successive generations. The people of Sanskrit and Dravidian traditions had their educational methods. Their Vedas, Puranas, the epics such as Ramayana and Mahabharata became educational tools. Their Sixty-Four Arts communicated specialized knowledge in medicine, astronomy, agriculture, war, trade, and the like. Additionally, the Buddhists and the Jains maintained their own centers of higher learning (e.g., the Nalanda University in Bihar). Their missionary efforts rejuvenated older languages such as Tamil and enriched them with new pieces of literature namely *Tholkappiyam* and *Silapathikaram*.

All these educational methods were contextual, periodical and opportunistic. Not all people had access to them. The people of the three Varnas, namely the Brahmins, Kshatriyas, and Vaishyas (i.e., the social orders of priests, rulers and traders) had access to knowledge, skills and wealth. The Sudras, i.e., the people of the fourth Varna, were viewed as a servile group; hence, their access to formal education was highly restricted. Among the Tamils, the social position of these Sudras was different. They controlled most temples, large tracts of lands, and constituted a political force. People who did not belong to this four-fold Varna had little or no access to formal education. They learned to perform the works of their *jati* ("birth group"); those groups that specialized in the maintenance of animals, meat production and consumption, removing, burying or cremating carcasses were branded as ritually impure and excluded from social upward mobility. The revival of Tamil bhakti religions from the 7th century onward recognized religious contributions by certain *Avarna* individuals, but it did not include all peoples of every social strata. People of other non-polluting *jatis* specialized in art, architecture, music, medicine, and other disciplines. None of these educational skills were standardized.

No one supervised their implementation in centers of education such as temples, religious mats, royal palaces, the veranda of homes, and the *gurukulas*. Imitation and memorization became two major modes of education. Tales, proverbs, riddles, and taboos told the people what they could do and what they should avoid. There were many *pulavars* (scholars), *pundits* (intellectuals), and *sastris* (professors) and these were only men and not women. Girls and women did not enjoy formal education. The *Devadasis* (servants of deities) and a few women in palaces or in aristocratic families had formal education in reading, writing and dancing. The public perception of the Devadasis was prostitutes, who should not be engaged in monogamous relationships, and as the *Nityasumangali* (the one who is perpetually blessed i.e., free from widowhood) they were kept away from any form of formal training in reading, writing, singing and dancing. At the same time, Indians valued motherhood greatly. Almost all of their male deities have a female counterpart. The virgin-goddess is normally portrayed as courageous, vengeful, blood-thirsty, and fearsome. Married goddess is domestic. Indians realized the importance of women in religious and domestic areas; however, they did not extend equal rights to women in educational spheres.

Dr. B. R. Ambedkar

The pre-reformation education in India had its own merits and areas for improvement, which Christian missionaries would attempt to address. Education could encourage the oppressed ones to fight and remove injustice and exploitation and pave ways for the free thinking. He recognized that lack of education was the main cause for the backwardness of poor people. Educate, agitate and organize are three final words of Dr. Ambedkar. According to Ambedkar one must get educated before he is conducting agitated thoughts for the movement, so that people can organize with his support.

A singular role that Ambedkar played in the upliftment of the untouchables in the early 20th century and the importance that he gave to modern education for their betterment deserves special emphasis. In conferences, lectures and also in meetings, Ambedkar encouraged untouchable youth to gain the education to raise their social status and image. His educational contribution starts on a wider scale of educating classes and masses. For Ambedkar, education was the main key to open the doors of light, vision and wisdom.

He said,

> Education is something which ought to be brought within the reach of everyone. The object of primary education is to see that every child that enters the portals of a primary school leaves it only at a stage when it becomes literate continuous to be literate throughout the rest of his life.

Martin Luther King

The need for educational reform was urgent at the beginning of the sixteenth century. There existed no school system and it often was limited to teaching the children of wealthy merchants and city rulers. In many places, the Roman Catholic Church supervised the training of the youth in monasteries, cloisters, and other church run institutions. But these were falling into disrepute and disrepair, as the populace reacted against the corruption and abuses monk and the clergy. Many parents stopped the training of their offspring, so that one of the first tasks of the reformers was to convince parents that the spiritual well-being of their children was more important than their physical comfort. Martin Luther was at the forefront of those who realized the need for change in education, and with characteristic zeal he sought to effect improvements in Wittenberg and throughout Germany. While he composed only a few works that treat education directly, his other writings often reveal an attempt to relate education to the doctrinal rediscoveries of the reformation. Luther's views would be much refined by pedagogues.

Alexander Duff

Later in the sixteenth century and beyond, many reformers and scholars provided a substantial basis for the further reform of education. Education, saturated with the teaching of the Scriptures, was the means to be used in bringing change. While religious instruction was of special significance, Alexander Duff aimed to teach every branch of useful knowledge, elementary forms at first, advancing to the highest levels of study in history, literature, logic, mental and moral philosophy, mathematics, biology, physics and other sciences. These aims differed greatly from those of other Christian educational institutions. After consulting with a wise Indian adviser, Duff resolved not to teach in Bengali, Persian, Arabic or Sanskrit but to use English as the medium of teaching. This meant that students using other languages were all learning English equally; they were taught the Scriptures in English, were introduced to English literature, much of which was permeated with the spirit of Christianity and studied the sciences in English, freed from the focus of the ideas that permeate Hindu thought.

Duff responded by recommending the following:

1. The gradual abolition of oriental colleges for the educational training of natives, liberating funds for the purposes of sound and healthful education.

2. The relinquishing of pecuniary control over primary or elementary education by the Government, thus achieving considerable saving.

3. That lectureships on high professional subjects such as law and civil engineering should be established on a free and unrestricted basis allowing attendance of qualified students from all other institutions and that, in Calcutta, a university might be established on the general model of London University, with enough faculties in such a way as to stimulate and foster studies in Government and non- Government institutions. The Government ought to extend its aid to all other institutions where sound general education is communicated.

4. It altered the policy of the government of India in educational matters.

William Carey

"Expect great things from God. Attempt great things for God", said William Carey.

Carey and Mrs. Marshman started schools for Indian boys and girls. The success of this school resulted in the establishment of the Calcutta Baptist Female School Society in 1819, and an additional school for started for girls in Calcutta. Free school for the low castes and the outcasts were always a chief feature of Carey's work, and these were started within a twenty-mile radius of Serampore where almost 8,000 children attended.

Conclusion

The classical Christian education position claims that children progress through three stages of development and that the three components of the trivium complement these natural learning stages. The first stage involves memorizing facts through chants, stories and songs. In the second stage, students learn how to argue and analyze by formal training in logic. The third stage focuses on learning to express knowledge persuasively and elegantly. When compared to the reformed understanding of covenant children and reformed purposes and methods of education, classical Christian education is found to be too intellectualistic and elitist to be compatible with a reformed Christian perspective on education.

Bibliography

An English translation is offered by C.M. Jacobs in Luther's Works. Vol. 46 (Philadelphia: 1967).

Duff, *Missions the Chief End*, 1839.

Madan T.N (Ed) 1991, *Religion in India*, Delhi: Oxford University press.

Nithya. P, *International Journal of Multidisciplinary Educational Research*, ISSN: 2277-7881 Vol 1, Issue 2, June 2012.

Ruth and Vishal Mangalwadi, *William Carey*, (Nivedit Good Books Distributors Private Limited, 1993).

Sayers, Dorothy, *The Lost Tools of Learning*, London: Routledge, Chapman, and Hall, Ltd.], 1947.

Sharma K.L, *"Stresses in Caste stratification"*, Economic and political weekly, volume.4, No.3.

Sinha, *Caste in India*, A Survey of Research in Sociology and Social Anthropology Vol.1, Bombay: Popular Prakashan.

7

Knowledge Expansion and Border Crossing:

A Paradigm Shift from Gurukula System to Digital Era

Umesh Samuel Jebaseelan

"Education is the most powerful weapon which you can use to change the world". - **Nelson Mandela**

The seeds of knowledge, during ancient times, were spiritual texts, sown in children at a very young age. Religious training and traditional knowledge were divulged orally and astute pre-teens and adolescents were trained to read these texts and enunciate *mantras* or *slokas* about God. The Zest for knowledge and the quest for the truth sprouted in their tender minds and they matured with a passion towards unearthing and garnering the mysteries of Mankind.

Education in this heritage-rich, ancient land, found its origins during the time of the sages and the gurus. Children were sent to these teachers and received all-round instruction which enhanced every aspect of the young minds and influenced every branch of their lives, equipping them in all fields - the religion, the scriptures, the philosophy, the literature, the warfare, the statecraft, medicine, astrology and the history.

Widely accepted as the first University in the World and dating back to 600 BC, Taxila, or Takshashila, was an early Hindu and Buddhist center of learning. The winds of time played to perfection, their role, in upgrading the curriculum as skills such as archery, hunting and elephant lore joined the existing law school, medical school and school of military science. Nalanda, yet another primordial institution, was established in the fifth century AD in Bihar and resolutely served the cause of education until 1200 AD. Although primarily devoted to Buddhist studies, subjects like fine arts, medicine, mathematics, astronomy, politics and the art of war constituted a major part of the academic structure.

The emergence of Islam in Hindustan created ripples of Islamic influence in traditional methods of education. The construction of educational institutions and universities was on the rise and the Islamic system placed emphasis on the connection between science and humanities. Private tutoring in India owes its existence to the Riyazis (tutors), the educated professionals of the middle ages, who earned their living by performing tasks such as creating calendars and generating revenue estimates for nobility.

The system stepped into its final stage of evolution – its current form – during the age of the British Raj. Aiming to provide modern education to the Indians, the colonizers introduced the use of English language into the curriculum.

Missionary Activists Charles Grant and William Wilberforce were the perseverant forerunners whotoddled towards their goal - to teach western literature and preach Christianity – and succeeded by initiating the dismantling of the non-intervention in education policy of the Company.

Lord Macaulay, a pioneer of the 20th century, then took up the reins and proposed that Education should be filtered from upper class to lower class to make it cost effective and to spread western education.

The East India Company's efforts in forging together a structure which remained unaltered by ancestral principles brought about a revolution in the realms of intellect and awakened a keen sense of rationality in the masses. The Calcutta Madrasa, Sanskrit College and Fort William College were the ripe harvests of their years of unstinted labor and selfless toil.

Teachers are artists and no artist can create masterpieces without his tools. As Education began to ascend on the priority list of the general public, the need for effective methods of teaching and interactive sources of instruction, proportionately, began to rise.

The Chalk and Talk method, (a monologue presentation done while the speaker draws), was the first of the initiatives to convert the classroom into interactive sessions. Students focused on the blackboard, the lecturer's voice and the actions they displayed. The written information, which the students could physically witness, served to enhance the memory of the listeners.

However, in an ever-changing world, a metamorphosis of methods was inevitable. Innovative means of schooling and the incorporation of technology were the answers to the issue of effective teaching. Overhead Projectors could display images to the audience and facilitated an easy low-cost interactive environment for Educators. The OHP's were the start of an evolving trend of technology-aided teaching methodologies.

LCD projectors, the futuristic, evolved form of the overhead projectors, later sauntered into the frame. High-resolution Images, Videos and data from computers could be directly projected on to flat surfaces and the LCD's soon became the most effective and prevalent methods of teaching. The most conservative and budget-conscious institutions have found the direct influence of the audial-visual effect on the students, increasingly attractive.

Cyber space and virtual reality have transformed the globe into a village, the world into a 'small place'. The field of Education has not been left uninfluenced by the invasion of the Internet. An online classroom, an interface where learners and instructors across the globe can collaborate, participate and interact on a level platform, is the most cost effective and befitting source of education.

Integrating and inculcating user-friendly learning interfaces like specialized software, audience response technology, assistive listening devices and networking audio/visual capabilities has fostered technology-enhanced classrooms. Smart classrooms provide direct access to the granaries and stockpiles of knowledge buried in the folds of the World Wide Web.

Online courses are revolutionizing formal education, and have opened a new avenue of outreach on cultural and scientific topics. These courses deliver a series of lessons to a web browser or mobile device, to be conveniently accessed anytime, anyplace. According to Sabri .G. Begawi, **Online education** is defined as the creation and proliferation of the personal computer, the globalization of ideas and other human acts, and the use of technology in exchanging ideas and providing access to more people.

ACADEMIC EXCELLENCE IN HIGHER EDUCATION – A BIRDS EYE VIEW

The Educational system in India has traversed the deserts of time and has mastered the art of being on par with global standards. The overseers, the accrediting bodies which reward and assess institutions within the borders of the country are, University Grants Commission (UGC), New Delhi, National Assessment and Accreditation Council (NAAC), Bengaluru and National Institutional Ranking Framework (NIRF) by Ministry of Human Resource Development (MHRD).

The judgement of the NAAC is based on the seven criteria identified by the Council. The NIRF constitutes five parameters which are set by a core committee recommended and formed by the Honorable Minister of Human Resource Development.

The Indian Rankings 2017 uncovered a remarkable fact – Of the top 10 colleges, 4 were Christian institutions. The feat remained undeterred and the Indian Rankings 2018 unveiled 3 Christian institutions in the College Category, one in the Medical ranking list and one among the top 10 management institutions in the nation.

Times Higher Education (THE) accredits institutions on a global scale. The THE World University Rankings are subject to independent audit by professional services firm, Prince Water house Coopers (PwC). Although judging is based on the 13 performance indicators as the global rankings, the Asia University Rankings are recalibrated to reflect the attributes of Asia's institutions.

The service of the benevolent and philanthropic missionaries and the altruistic Christians of the East India Company have left an ineradicable mark on the history of education and development in India. Stepping in the marks of their soles, embedded in the sands of time, Christian institutions, today, are striving to extend their selfless service and be heralded amongst the best universities of India.

To extend the greatest impact among the student community, according to LINDA KARDAMIS, Christian teachers must

1. Have a strong sense of mission
2. Strive for excellence
3. Love your students
4. Teach for the heart (not just outward behavior)
5. Be humble and real
6. Encourage and edify those around us
7. Develop a strong relationship with God

8. Seek wisdom and truth by thinking Biblically

9. Trust God and not be afraid

10. Be evidences of the fruits of the spirit

It can be wrapped up that, even in the cutting edge of technology; education with ethical and moral values instigated by the Christian institutions is highly laudable.

References

De Vries, Marc J. (2018).Handbook of Technology Education.(Ed.), Springer

Eleanor Ann Daniel, John William Wade(1999). Foundations for Christian Education, College Press.

Indra Sharma, Sharma N.R. (1984) History and Problems of Indian Education. N.R.Sharma Vinod Pusthak Mandir, Agra.

Leonard D.L (1895). A Hundred Years of Missions, New York.

Naik J.P and Syed Nurullah(1975).Students History of Education in India. New Delhi.

Sharan, Bishambhar (1968). The Gurukula System of Education In India & Its Application to Modern Times (Abridged Edition). Amazon. com: Books.

Yogendra K.Sharma (2001).History and Problem of Education" vol II Kanishka Publishers and Distributors, New Delhi.

Websites

https://www.educationworld.in/relevance-of-modern-gurukul-system-in-new-india/

https://askopinion.com/gurukul-system-of-education-vs-modern-education-system

https://www.google.com/search?q=gurukul+system+of+education+vs+modern+education&oq=g&aqs=chrome. 4.69i57j0l3j35i39j69i60.3426j1j8&sourceid=chrome&ie=UTF-8

http://www.shareyouressays.com/knowledge/7-most-important-aims-of-education-for-the-students-in-the-gurukul-upanishadic-philosophy/111859

https://www.ijarse.com/images/fullpdf/1426573415_815.pdf

8

Rethinking Education in Today's Context in Pursuit of Alternative Ideas and Imagination: Making Education Accessible

Jacob Swamynathan

"Education is not the learning of facts, but the training of the mind to think" - **Albert Einstein**

The importance of educational reforms is required to be understood on periodic intervals for upgrading the standards of learning. When the reforms are not considered upon proper assessments, it might lead to an ignorant generation growing to build a nonproductive society. On a larger perceptive, Educational reforms leads to social reforms. We can date back our education system to centuries earlier, where we would have noticed that the education was in art forms and findings through the education were documented in writing. As days passed through, we have moved on from educating through writing and documentation in art forms. The Education system we ensue dates to 18th Century where the platform for learning was not available to everyone. It was restricted to only few segments of the society. Harvard University decided the 12 years of Early Elementary

Education scheme in 1892, after which there has been no consideration for further reformation in this model.

In this model, the standardization test is based on the memory skills that the child has endowed with and we fail to understand that the capability of recollection varies from individual to individual, owing to a lot of factors. This leads to an unhealthy design of a Child's growth with the atmosphere of failure around. Instead, the Standardization Model should be based on the character, integrity and behavioral confidence that the child demonstrates. This, in turn, will enable the child to grow in an optimistic atmosphere.

"The Mind is not a vessel that needs filling, but wood that needs igniting." - Plutarch

Further, the aspects of understanding the world through somebody's perceptive may kill the originality of a student. We have seen in history that only those who have questioned the "Why's" have gone past the "Is". We assume that planting words into the mind of learners makes them educated. What we discount is the usage of those words in practicality which will make a difference.

We should therefore move into the atmosphere of teaching students on practical demonstration of lubricated knowledge. Each subject that the child learns through worded text should be structured to make them understand the practical "do how" which helps the world evolve.

Are we making them Imaginative?

We would have recognized, as a child grows, that they tend to lose out on imagination which they had utilized during the early infant age. We must accept the fact that each of our imagination is not the same as other. It is unique and different. Respecting a child's imagination is a way that we can nurture the creativity in them. Let the child learn science through the way they look at it. Doing so, the child builds an independent thought process within and can face his/ her challenging situations of life with ease. Let the child write down his/her own theory on what he/she has learned; let the child examine them based on what he/ she has understood and not on what the child has memorized.

Are we skilling them enough?

Right through from the kindergarten to their graduating out of Matric School, we have successfully skilled them with the power of memorizing texts. This has made a child assume or put in context to misunderstand that if he/ she does not possess memory skills, they are labelled are failures. As such, medically, we understand that as we age our brain memory shrinks. So, should we term all the elderly and aged as failures? This is where empowering them and equipping them with the needed skills in the area of their interest makes a difference. Anything that you love doing, need not be memorized. It just happens with spontaneity.

Again, being on auto mode need not be interesting. For example, the brushing of teeth daily is an on- going process and needs no memory skills to do, however do we need passion to do it? Not really. But when it comes to learning, passion is the fuel to understand your liking and adapting to the skill you like to possess. Check the child's interest. This will guide you to observe what they might be interested in. If a Child loves painting, anything that you want to teach a child, use the technique of painting and that will help.

What can be taught in our Institutes?

- Let them learn Math by knowing the economics of home.

- Let them learn Social Science not by learning Histories but by adapting to know behavioral patterns in Social gathering.

- Let them Learn Geography by learning to respect cultural differences rather than learning comparable statistics.

- Let them learn Algebra by learning the science behind Business.

- Let them learn Biology by learning the healthy habits of living.

Are we making them aware of what is happening around them?

Awareness is the important key for a child to be innovative and creative. In today's world, technology has become smart and has made the user less intelligent. There rises an important question. Do our students understand the happenings around them? When their ignorance towards the socio-political happenings is on rise, we could witness the discrimination against their growth considerably inclined; right from the effigy of corruption, sexual exploitation and abuse of a child.

Being aware of these challenges in today's world is what the child must be educated on. Special focus on confidence building, overcoming failures, being against social evils, fighting sexual abuse is the need of the hour in our education system. This is what the child faces in the unseen, unknown and unpredictable world. Once they are promoted with the awareness to tackle these challenges, learning to score more in the text mode of learning becomes un-demanded. Possibly the best learning atmosphere is where the child understands his/ her value and cherish his/ her unique individuality.

When you accomplish this vision, the child realizes his/ her value; the child will begin to enjoy his/ her strengths and in turn, will continue to equip and be nurtured towards positive developments. This can be induced by teaching them good moral values. In our present context, where teaching Moral Science in classrooms is considered out dated and of old school culture, teachers should make it a point to have good values taught in the class through scriptural stories. It is not about preaching religion but teaching about what makes you the potential human that God created you for. Teaching them on how to have a healthy child - parent relationship is also the need of the hour. The child should always feel a sense of I'M HEARD. This will help the child feel secured.

Are we inclusive in our education system?

The main objective of education is to empower humans. However, there lays a question unanswered - Are we inclusive in this process? Most of the unnoticed segments of this society have been yearning to have this boon called education to enlighten their senses. One of the segments is that of the people with disabilities. In a World, where disabled are considered outcast and helpless, Education remains a distant dream for many of them with physical challenges. As education providers, we have seen ourselves shunning away from having them in closeness citing the infrastructure failure in our education system. The main source of empowering the disabled is providing accessibility to education. As a society, we have deprived them the rights to learn. Their aspirations is as much skin and alike us. They love to be in classrooms, playgrounds, labs and library that we like to be in. Understanding their needs, we ought to be sensitive towards an inclusive society. This will help them to improve economically, socially and mentally. Few pointers to be considered are as follows:

- They have the right to study and experience learning.

- They must be provided accessibility to every port in the learning arena.

- They must be considered equals. This will alone enhance their sense of belonging in the society.

- Respect the skills. They might be different, but they too have skills.

- Make them feel important and they play a positive part in building the nation.

  Getting hold of the difficulty deep down is what is hard. Because if it is grasped near the surface it simply remains the difficulty it was. It has to be pulled out by the roots; and that involves our beginning to think in a new way. The change is as decisive as, for example, that from the alchemical to the chemical way of thinking. The new way of thinking is what is so hard to establish. Once the new way of thinking has been established, the old problems vanish; indeed, they become hard to recapture. For they go with our way of expressing ourselves and, if we clothe ourselves in a new form of expression, the old problems are discarded along with the old garment. – Wittgenstein, 1984

9

Rethinking Ecclesia-Empowerment and Education Perspective:

Education is for Transformation: Towards a Borderless Church

C.R. Vincent

Greetings to you all in the matchless name of our Lord and Saviour Jesus Christ from the South Kerala Diocese. At the very outset, let me express my deep appreciation and thanks to Dr. Radnakara Sathanantha and Rev. Solomon Paul, Director of Youth Department, for this privilege of addressing this convened gathering. As a proud member of the Church of South India and being a Pastor, I am glad to express my gratitude to this great church for being such an important part of my formation as a Christian, serving the ecumenical movement.

Let me now come to the theme of this consultation, "Transformation of people through Education". What a bold declaration! What a challenging sign of hope that in Christ, we can claim "transformation of life", not just for some, but for all! This is the gift of our faith that we can offer to India and to the world. Choosing this theme for this particular consultation is important because of the present context in which we are called to be church in our world and in India today.

There were a lot of educational commissions which led to the social growth and development of our nation *before independence*. In 1813, the East India Company started to educate the Indians in English language, which helped the Indians to know the social and cultural outlook towards the Western culture. The famous Macaulay's Minutes in 1835 was a turning point for the educational development of India. Though Macaulay's sole ambition was to create a community of Anglo Indian on the basis of complexion, patriotism, thought, aspirations and even by blood, it paved the way for the self-awareness which also helped for the transformation of the people. Wood's despatch (1854), the famous 'Magna Carta' of Indian education, helped to formulate the first national education policy of India. Following that, the other education commissions which helped for the transformation of the then Indian society were:

- ➢ Hunter commission in 1882

- ➢ University commissions of 1902 and 1917[1]

The reports which analysed on the social problems and which were responsible for bringing out the ability in students to solve them is also of utmost importance. These reports focussed on 'life centred' education to be given to children and adopted many principles from Mahatma Gandhi's 'Vardha Plan' of 1937.

After the independence of our nation, the educational system took its shape with the national aims. This was practically implemented through the following commissions:

- ➢ University Education Commission or Radhakrishnan Commission (1948-'49)

- ➢ Secondary Education commission or Muthaliyar commission (1952-'53)

> ➤ Education commission or Kothari commission (1964-'62)[2]

The Kothari commission on Education says, "The destiny of India is now being shaped in her class-rooms". Here the role of church on education in formal system is important. Long years ago, the foreigners from abroad came to India and to the other south-eastern countries. Their aim was to make trade with those countries and to earn as much as profits. Following the foreigners, Christian missionaries came to India and to the other parts of the continent. They wanted to preach the people with Gospel works. They soon realised the fact that most of the people were ignorant and illiterate and they lacked education. They felt that their task of preaching Gospel to them is not an easy one. The rulers and native kings in power in those days had done nothing in the case of imparting knowledge or educating the poor.

Hence, the missionaries had to take care of the task of educating the poor. A large majority of the weaker sections of the people, especially the fishermen were deprived of education because of the caste system prevailed in those days with certain other inequalities. In India, 'Higher Education' faces many challenges, even today. The Grants commission which was established by the Indian Parliament Act of 1956, began to take steps for bettering the quality of higher education. Through the same Act, National Accreditation and Assessment Council (NAAC) was also established. Based on certain well defined criteria, NAAC gave recognition and affiliation to educational institutions for higher studies. Although there are many disputes and issues on this matter, without any doubt, this paved the way for social development through education. Education transformed their lives. Knowledge opened their eyes to their rights and individual freedom. Education broadened their horizon. The freedom that education brought enhanced their social, cultural, economical and spiritual life. It was breath of fresh, cleansing air that brought life and light to the almost dead souls. The church provided them the haven they needed.

But now, we live in an India of grave contradictions, where globalisation as a deliberate political project has sustained inequalities and fragmentation and untold poverty and sufferings for the many. On the other hand, it has given space for the growth of grotesque expressions of consumerism and wealth in the hands of a few. India is hailed as a success story in economic growth and development, for instance by the World Bank-but what we often overlook is the fact that the development of India is at a heavy and unjust price that millions of the poor have to pay, as they are excluded from enjoying the fruits of progress. We live in a world and in India where violence and injustice are the norm. We live in a world where war seems to be a readily available weapon in the hands of insolent might. We live in an India where, in the name of religion and religious identity, some of the most heinous acts of violence are committed. We live in an India where in the name of caste superiority, a form of genocide is quietly being committed against the Dalits. I call it quiet, because we have not yet acknowledged that the atrocities committed against the Dalits, which so often leads to the massacre of innocents is a form of genocide against a whole world of people. We live in an India where violence against women is on the increase, according to Government of India statistics, and this has not been taken seriously enough even by the church. The media and advertising is one of the most powerful and influential agent of socialisation in modern context. We need to critique how media promote gender roles in full form. There is a need to educate people to promote gender equality and partnership through media education. Schools and other educational institutions should also be an active agent in promoting gender justice education by restructuring the whole curricula. Cultural education should be also developed with fair gender justice.

It is in such a context that we today boldly assert as the Church of South India that education is for the transformation of life. When we make such an assertion, of course, it goes with the commitment that we will do all we can to bring this promise to action, committing ourselves to act on behalf of all those who are in the periphery of our societies, struggling somehow to survive. If this is our commitment then, the next challenge is for us to discern if there is anything that boarders us as a church. What, if any, are the obstacles that lie in the way of our witness and service to the people of India for transformation? Is it once again the opportune moment for an analytical look at the life and witness of the CSI? Forgive me for saying this, but I say it as someone who loves this church, I sometimes feel ashamed that we have carried into the church, caste, politics and all that is unhealthy and corrupt in the political systems that exist in the country. Let us pray for God' s guidance that we will as leaders, steer the church into its ordained role in our country and world today. The theme of this meeting on education and empowerment challenges us to discover what we can contribute to the realisation that in Christ, the transformation can be achieved through Christian education.

Still, why Christian education?

* More than a billion people World-wide live on less than $1/day.

* 2.73 billion people worldwide live below the official world poverty line: $2/day.[3]

* There are 72 million school age children who are not in school worldwide. And these numbers are much lower than the reality, since many students who are enrolled do not attend for a variety of reasons like:[4]

    - A lot of children simply live a long way from school. Four out of five children who do not go to school live in rural areas.[5]

    - 166 million children between the age of 5 and 14 years have to work- often up to 16 hours a day.[6]

    - Can't afford essentials- Tuition may be free, but can't afford the fees required for uniforms and supplies.

The Church of South India: Its intentions and hope for transformation

In preparation for this paper, I read, once again, Rajaiah D Paul's penetrating analysis of life of the CSI, in the book, "Ecumenism in action: A Historical Survey of the Church of South India". The author in this book speaks of the CSI as "the result of obedience", because in his understanding, "unity is the will of God" and "disunity is sin."[7] To him the unity of the church is a necessary prerequisite for our witness in a "non –Christian" world to transform the current scenario. But for this, he strongly believed that "the church of Christ in India should become distinctly and unmistakably Indian." But underlying the book is his concern about the Church's excessive dependence on foreign help for its ministries. He goes on further and expresses his regret that, "the church in this country is a mere replica of Western Churches." When highlighting the problems the church faces, he speaks of "our inherited faith, which does involve a personal commitment in the case of a great many of its followers", in the field of education.

At present, Christian education by and large refers to the Sunday School, which is structured in the pattern of the schools of general education. There the actual learning period is not more than one hour. During this one hour a week program, several ideas, values and articles of faith are deposited in the minds of the learners. It is the Church or the Community of Faith (Macrocosm) with the Christian family (microcosm) that forms the base community or a nursery where the Christian style of life is experimented. Only in the church and the family, will the children and youth be able to imitate the adult leaders and internalise their role models. This calls for a conscious training of natural leaders in the Church and homes.

Thus, the Church of South India implements its hopes and intentions for transformation through education mainly via Sunday School and also via its own educational institutions.

The challenges ahead in view to transformation

First of all, I hope that we will have the courage to once again engage in an intensive study and critique of the church so that we can re-define more clearly what its missionary tasks need to be for today. We need to constantly and honestly review our success stories, boldly acclaim them and be proud of the achievements we have made. Here we can acknowledge once again the gift of organic unity which is at the heart of the CSI. I would also lift up as important, the contributions by the members of the CSI church like Bishop Samuel Amrithem and Bishop Azariah and so on to the world church and to the ecumenical movement-as renowned theologians and leaders.

But then, it is equally important and necessary that we also remind ourselves of where we have failed to be the church of Christ in India today. Such honesty is essential if we are to make our witness relevant and if we are to contribute to transformation of the injustices in our society and in the world. It noticed that most of our educational systems focus only on the "dos" and "do nots". And even those children that are in school often receive a poor education as classrooms are overcrowded and teachers are underqualified. But only when the children and youth are educated to wrestle with environmental, social and economic issues that affect the present and future of the Church and society, will they use their God-given potentialities and begin to think critically, biblically and theologically to find a suitable faith response and contemplate action. Let us attempt to begin to describe some areas in which we partly or completely failed in the gone days, so that we can rectify them and live up to the commitment to ensure education for transformation.

❖ *Transforming our ministries of care and service*

What we need in India today is transformative justice that can be enjoyed by all those who have been excluded and thus denied the joys of education. This demands a re-look at the ways we have served our people thus far. With globalisation process, has come the commercialisation of education, health care and even social welfare services. These have traditionally been the domain of the ministry and contributions of the church. In fact we are aware that the Church's healthcare and educational programmes had inspired the governments and others efforts in the last century-the churches provided model. And yet today, in the name of efficiency and professionalism have we also, as church institutions, slowly alienated ourselves from those who cannot afford the educational and other welfare services that we offer? Let us then, first transform ourselves and commit for this purpose, according to our call, without expecting anything in return, but hoping only for the crown of glory that our Saviour has in hand for us. I believe that there are still many areas in which the church is desperately needed. To give just one example, we could do so much more for those who are slowly dying due to HIV-AIDS, cancer and other chronic diseases. Sadly, the view of the society is that, only a few are called to be the channels of hope and relief for these victims. The church has to move beyond moral condemnation and respond with love and concern. The church should provide education to the public as well as care and support for the victims. What a powerful testimony of witness and service this will be to India and to the world church!

❖ *Restructuring Christian education*

As an activity of God's redemption, Christian Educational ministry is to enable, facilitate and empower the members of Christian faith community, so that the believers are made conscious, alert and attentive to God's praxis not only in the church but also in the society, which closely relates to God's emancipating activity in the world.[8] Education is an effective tool to perpetuate the oppressive structure or can be dynamic to bring transformation upon the people. Christian education should be used to transform the community and to remove any disparity. For this, there is a need to restructure educational ministry of our churches. Sunday school which is the backbone of Christian education in the church needs a thorough revision which is still running in traditional paradigm, conservative in its contents and approaches. We need to think critically our liturgies of worship, content of preaching and witness in mission to transform. We should make it a must that the congregation should experience the heavenly joy that is available for free through the cross, in our worship sessions, through the transformation of liturgies, songs and so on to ease the process of transformation. Being a Pastor, I have heard people complaining often about not being able to understand the sermons which are interspersed with surplus theological principles. Hence, efforts should be made to simplify the Good news and convey impart it to the people so that it will transform them.

❖ *Becoming reconciling and healing communities*

It is important to remind ourselves again of how difficult life is becoming in our country because of the growing religious atrocities, fundamentalisms, and aggressive tactics of the so called dominant groups. From my conversations with many ordinary Christians I recognise just how threatened they feel in India today and the discrimination they experienced is beyond imagination but real as well, in their lives. In such a context it sounds presumptuous to call on congregations to become healing and reconciling communities, so that we could live in peace and harmony amongst ourselves and also with our neighbours. However, we have no choice if we are to be true to the gospel. It is in this aspect the Christian Education outranks other educational systems by educating an individual to forgive and to forget just as Christ did. The mainline churches such as the CSI should take a lead in imparting these educational values to transform our communities into a healing and reconciling one. The need of the hour in the current scenario is a healing hand to encounter all the hatred and violence that is being promoted by the hardliners in all religions. We have, as Christians in this country, for too long hidden behind our minority status in order to legitimise our inaction and silence when we see forms of injustice. But, as Dr.K.Rajaratnam, Lutheran church leader reminds us, "the true church is a minority. Both conceptually and structurally, the church should always be a minority, because a prophetic church can only be a minority. The church which serves the whole world as salt, leaven and the light of the world is a minority functionally." Being salt, leaven and light is the way for us Christians to bring about transformation.

❖ *Envisioning the church in the original term of Ecclesia*
The church is a community of believers; it is not a cultural organisation.[9] It is an inclusive community of equals gathered together on the basis of faith in Christ. It should be a community where everyone irrespective of gender, race, ethnic, rich or poor, disabled or abled will be accepted, appreciate the differences and uniqueness of every individual. Church should be a community where sharing of love and peace and unity is practiced. It should be a community of equals where leadership is shared equally and participate equally. Christian education in church is to be perceived as ecumenical education. Ecumenical Education implies progressing towards holistic spirituality, provided with the tools of critical consciousness to see how reality is being detained to be empowered and to act for social transformation in par with the prophetic witness of the good news.[10]

Plurality or pluralism is a notion, which is gaining increasing attention in the discussions of Mission of God. The stress is on creating one human community in the midst of diverse religious traditions. Plurality is God's created design for humankind and it is in coexistence that we discover the beauty and richness of plurality. As for our role model, Christ, the whole humankind with diversity and plurality assumes significance and hence, in all his dealings with people, he upheld this principle of common humanity very emphatically. To him, all, irrespective of differences are equal in the sight of God. So, he did not have any hesitation to move with the lowly and downtrodden. Now, this is an example set for the church today.

Impacts of Education in general

Individuals

Learning to read, do simple math, reason and communicate helps people make informed choices about their lives and begins to break the cycle of poverty, one person at a time.

Health

Educated mothers have healthier children because they are more likely to understand and use prenatal care, assisted childbirth and postnatal care, as well as immunize their children.

Young people who have completed primary education are less than half as likely to contract HIV-AIDS. Education prepares and enables them to know and understand how to prevent diseases and to utilize the health services available.

Economy

Each additional year of schooling often translates into 10% higher wages. No country has ever achieved significant, continuous and rapid growth without reaching an adult literacy rate of at least 40%.

Society

Education supports the growth of civil society, democracy and political stability, allowing people to learn about their rights and acquire their rights and acquire the skills and knowledge necessary to exercise them. It also contributes to environmental sustainability, helping people make decisions today that don't compromise the needs of future generations.

Education for Transformation

In the book of prophet Jeremiah, in chapter 18, verses from 1-6, our Lord is depicted as a potter who can transform and mould anything or anyone to what seems 'best to Him.' Dear brothers and sisters in Christ, it is now our duty as we are entrusted with the sacred mission of sharing the Good news to the world, to carry out this transformation. Christian education was the best method for this transformation in the past and will also be effective in the future. Christian education is a Christ-centred one, which can transform our society and nation. The Catholic theologian Samuel Ryan says that the transformed 'In-Christ' experience demands a new world, new life-styles, new activities, a new network of relationships - in short, it demands radical newness. Educational psychological studies further supports this. S.K Mangal says, "The physical and socio-cultural environment of the individual needs to be modified in such a way that he may not be subjected to further disharmony and maladjustment."[11] Even when we emphasize on how amazing and effective education is, it cannot bring a deep, sweeping and everlasting change. Only a transformed heart can do that. Only God can transform hearts. We are as the Church of South India, is the child of Resurrected Jesus who I know is with us today, giving his grace, love and passion to transform ourselves into a Church that not just says that we will transform through Christian Education- but will live in this truth and act accordingly. What we need in India today is a prophetic leadership that would bring about an awareness about social and economic injustices in the country and equip the children, youth and adults to be agents of 'Shalom-God's coming Kingdom' in their own local situations. Hence the children and youth have to be exposed to concrete human situations to see the suffering masses and begin to raise questions. My prayer and hope is that the God of grace will transform us, our nation and the world. Let us strive relentlessly to achieve this goal. Thank you.

Endnotes

[1] Madhavan Nair S, 'Vidhyabyasam-Charithravum Shasthravum' (Thrissur:Breeze Publications,1995) pp 10-16.

[2] Madhavan Nair S, 'Vidhyabyasam-Charithravum Shasthravum' (Thrissur:Breeze Publications,1995) pp 17-31.

[3] Source:globalissues.org

[4] Source: worldbank.org

[5] Source: Federal Ministry for Economic Cooperation and Development, Germany

[6] Source: ILO- International Labour Organisation

[7] Rajaiah D. Paul, Eumenism in Action: A Historical Survey of the Church of South India. (Madras: CLS Press, 1972) pp 11-12.

[8] Mary Elizabeth Moore, Education for Continuity and Change (Nashvelli: Abingdon Press,1983), pp 60-61 .

[9] Limatula Longkumer, Christian Education for Transformation, Kolkata, Bishop's College, 2107, p 243.

[10] Samson Prabhakar, "Towards a Religious Education for an Inclusive Community," Bangalore Theological Forum XXVIII, no.3&4 (1996): 39.

[11] S.K. Mangal, Advanced Educational Psychology, New Delhi, [Published by Asoke K Ghosh, Prentice-Hall of India Private Limited,1993], p 30.

10

Beyond Christian Education:
Towards a Borderless Community
T. I. James

Introduction

What makes Christian Education distinct from Secular Education? Howard George Hendricks, a longtime professor at Dallas Theological Seminary says, *"Secular education seeks to make more successful and intelligent people. The Christian educator aspires to nothing less than the transformation of a believer (person) into the image of Christ."* I was working with CSI synod in the department of Pastoral Concern as its director and the predecessor of the present director, Rev. Cecil James Victor. I had to take care of Pastoral Aid Department, Youth Department and Department of Christian Education. As a part of that, I could do several programs for Christian Educators and Children. I enjoyed it very well. From the last December onwards, the Diocese of Malabar had entrusted me with another responsibility of managing the aided schools in our Diocese. We have 48 aided schools, i.e., funded by Kerala Government. Some are functioning very well and some others are not. The range of our diocesan schools is from 4000 students to 4 students. There is one school functioning with only 4 students. Last year it was 1 student and 1 Teacher. Now it is increased by 400%.

When I started this ministry as the Manager of Schools, I could recognize the fact that the present ministry of the Manger of Aided Schools and the former responsibility as the director of, including Christian Education department are not much different. At the synod level when I was working, I considered it as Children ministry among the children within the four walls of the Church; now, it is again Children Ministry but without boundaries. Our Mission Schools, Christian Colleges and Higher Education institutions provide a greater avenue to carry out children and youth ministry. It is necessary that we ponder upon the purpose of Christian Institutions in the Secular Society.

Firstly, let us formulate a relevant definition for Education without segregating Secular or Christian Education. According to Thomas Raymont (1906):

> Education in the narrow sense does not include self-culture and the general influences of one's surroundings, but only those special influences which are consciously and designedly brought to bear upon the youngsters by the adult persons of the community whether through the family, the church or the state.

The process of education takes place in social settings, and society as a whole exercises great control over its process. Every society uses education as a means for promoting its own interests. While education is subjected to the control of society, it also influences society by contributing to its goals. Education performs a threefold social function by maintaining, transmitting and creating social values, ideals, beliefs and culture. The values, ideals, goals, morals, traditions and culture of the society are inculcated in a child through education in order to make him/her an effective member of the society.

Even though this is the common goal and purpose of the Education, we can see that there are boundaries. The relevant question that arises here is, who draws the boundary line. In the present Indian scenario, it is very well noted that the threat of saffronisation has already intruded into our educational system. From the history, it can be inferred that different leaders/rulers had different views on education, and they molded the educational system according to their needs and necessities. As Nelson Mandela correctly pointed, *"Education is the most powerful weapon which you can use to change the world"*. Many rulers in the past proved that the quote of Nelson Mandela is correct. It is seen from the past to the present that education practices and its system changes according to the will of the rulers/leaders. Positive changes obviously strengthened the system and the others, deteriorated the efficiency of the education.

If we go through two examples from the history of missions, we can see it is true. Rulers have their own bias and they always use education as a weapon to implement their own agenda. Even in the history of Evangelization, it is evident. For example: If we search online for **the Letter from King Leopold II of Belgium to Colonial Missionaries, 1883,** we will get the evidence. You can easily understand the bias.

> You will go certainly to evangelize, but your evangelization must inspire above all Belgium interests. Your principal objective in our mission … is never to teach them (niggers) to know God, this they know already. …Your essential role is to facilitate the task of administrators and industrials, which means you will go to interpret the gospel in the way it will be the best to protect your interests in that part of the world. For these things, you have to keep watch on disinteresting our savages from the richness that is plenty [in their underground. To avoid that, they get interested in it, and make you murderous] competition and dream one day to overthrow you. Your knowledge of the gospel will allow you to find texts ordering, and encouraging your followers to love poverty, like "Happier are the poor because they will inherit the heaven" and, "It's very difficult for the rich to enter the kingdom of God." You have to detach from them and make them disrespect everything which gives courage to affront us. … Your action will be directed essentially to the younger ones, for they won't revolt when the recommendation of the priest is contradictory to their parent's teachings. The children have to

learn to obey what the missionary recommends, who is the father of their soul. You must singularly insist on their total submission and obedience, avoid developing the spirit in the schools, teach students to read and not to reason. ... Evangelize them (niggers) so that they stay forever in submission to the white colonialists, so they never revolt against the restraints they are undergoing. Recite every day – "Happy are those who are weeping because the kingdom of God is for them.

Another example from the Indian British colonial history is Macaulay's minute on Indian Education which is stated as follows:

...to attempt to educate the body of the people. We must at present do our best to form a class who may be interpreters between us and the millions whom we govern; a class of persons, Indian in blood and colour, but English in taste, in opinions, in morals, and in intellect. To that class we may leave it to refine the vernacular dialects of the country, to enrich those dialects with terms of science borrowed from the Western nomenclature, and to render them by degrees fit vehicles for conveying knowledge to the great mass of the population.

The initial policies introduced by the East India Company promoted an elitist English education geared towards a small minority of the population—the higher castes and classes. An important goal of these policies was to *"form a class of people who may be interpreters between us [the British] and the millions whom we govern, a class of persons Indian in blood and color, but English in taste, in opinion, in morals and intellect."* The hope was that this learned class would then enrich the vernacular languages and educate the masses, while providing a steady labor supply to the colonial administrative offices. British used education as the tool to change the colonial world as per their agenda. There is no doubt in that. The history repeats today in the regime of Narendra Modi and the propagators of *Hindutva*.

This is a great challenge before us from the time immemorial. Rulers used education as a tool for their convenience, on the one hand.

This will continue. Nobody can stop this. But within this context, how can we use Education as a tool for change is the major question that we should engage with. The missionaries, on the other hand, did not consider themselves as the agents of the colonial power; their primary purpose was the propagation of the gospel. Thus, it can be assumed that Christian missions and the government were in India for their own objectives, each found the other useful and functional. Government found the missions useful, in appeasing the hills tribes and providing education at a minimal cost to the people; the missions found the government useful in endorsing, in many cases, their educational work and in providing security for both themselves and their converts. Therefore, the relationship between the missions and the government can best described as co-operation in certain limited areas of mutual coincidence of interests.

Even though this was the fact in the context of the mission history, we can see other side also in the Mission History. We must learn from the history of our mission institutions as how the missionaries survived from such political directions of the colonial rulers. There are some positive signs also. The Mission Institutions stood firm on some noble ideals to uphold the inclusive attitude towards everyone. For example, the motto of Malabar Christian College, Calicut is Education without discrimination. The people who studied in this eminent institution for the last many decades, appraise the great missionaries for giving them such a great insight about a community beyond discrimination. This vision about a borderless Community, they have been receiving since the establishment of this College in 1848. In other words, the purpose of Christian Education or Christian college education or mission school education is to give a vision to the students, a vision of a borderless community.

The task for those who are teaching and managing such Schools and Higher Education institutions is that they should continue this vision of borderless church and border community. It is important that we understand the need to have similar goals in Christian Education as well as secular education in the Christian Colleges and Mission Schools.

Beyond Christian Education: Some Reflections

Let me also high light some reflection on what beyond Christian Education. The four components of Education and Christian Education are- a) Context b) Content c) Methods d) Outcomes. I would like to suggest a few points in the present day curriculum of Christian Education/ Sunday School to equip the young generation understand Church as a journey towards a borderless community. Strengthening leadership in the Church of South India necessitates that Christian education is done being 'mindful' of the vision and the mission of the Church. My humble opinion is that we are at the crossroads which calls for the shift of focus.

a.   Context: From Class room to the Community

At present, Christian education by and large refers to the Sunday School, that is structured in the pattern of the schools of general education. The actual learning period includes not more than one hour. During this one hour a week program, several ideas, values and articles of faith are deposited in the minds of the learners. Often, the growing person does not know how to act-out her/his faith. It is the Church or the Community of Faith (Macrocosm) with the Christian family (Microcosm) that forms the base community or a nursery where the Christian style of life is experimented. Only in the Church and in the family, the children and youth will be able to imitate the adult leaders and internalize their role models. This calls for a conscious training of natural leaders in the Church and homes.

b.   Content: From Information to Issues

It has been noticed that in many Sunday School sessions, attention is paid to the "Dos" and "Do nots" Even though songs, choruses, stories and memory verses are taught in the Sunday Schools, the bottom line is a pious or Holy-Holy behavior, to earn reputation as a "good girl" or a "good boy". Only when children and youth are educated to wrestle with environmental, social and economic issues that affect the present and future of the Church and Society, they would not only use their God-given potentialities, but also begin to think critically, biblically and theologically to find a suitable faith response and contemplate action. This engagement would also give opportunities for the leaders/facilitators to raise their level of theological thinking and to identify and develop leadership among those of the younger generation.

c.   Methods: From Head to Heart

For a long time, instructional methods took in to account mainly the intellectual abilities of the children-youth-adults. Remembering, analyzing, critiquing, understanding, imagining and reflecting have come to occupy a central place in teaching - learning processes. It is forgotten that human beings have a heart that feels and one's life style is very much controlled by her/his feelings. Hence, strengthening leadership in the Church involves concentrating on the attitudes, prejudices, dispositions and values of the learners. Even at a tender age, not only the struggle but also the contribution of great leaders could challenge the learners and motivate them to step in to their shoes as it were. A sense of commitment to the missiological vision of the Church and the passion to see the CSI emerging as a vibrant missionary movement in India must come from one's heart.

d.   Outcomes: From Knowledge to Prophetic Perspective.

On many occasions, parents, Sunday School teachers and Church elders, teachers in our Christian institutions feel comfortable when the children answer or reproduce correctly whatever is taught in the general assembly or class sessions of the Sunday School/Vacation Bible School or in Secular school. Further, the emphasis has been on memorization. This is due to the imported models of Christian education from the

West decades ago. On many occasions, it is forgotten that this model is value-based and culturally conditioned. What we need in India today is a prophetic leadership that would bring an awareness about social and economic injustices in the country and equip the children, youth and adults to be agents of *Shalom* – 'God's coming Kingdom' in their own local situations. Hence, children and youth have to be exposed to concrete human situations to see the suffering masses and begin to ask questions. Thus, they can be trained as future leaders in the Church and the society at large.

Rethinking the Healing of Mind in Today's Context towards a Borderless Church

Thyaline Thiagarajah

My views on healing come very much from my experience of living for thirty years in the war zone of Sri Lanka's civil war. For I have suffered the trauma of war with our people and I would say I have experienced post-traumatic stress disorder as a result of living in a war zone. I have also worked with our people who have suffered much due to the war and the tsunami, and especially in the camps for internally displaced people at the end of the civil war and in the northern regions of Sri Lanka that have borne the brunt of this war's brutality.

It was in the immediate aftermath of the war, as I began helping the people with the aid of a few of our pastors, that I realised the church response could not be limited to one form or modality. Every aspect of people's lives had been shattered and the destruction you might say was borderless. The physical, emotional, psychological and spiritual dimensions of the people's lives had suffered the violence, and if we were to respond we needed a centre or institution for holistic healing. Because everything in their lives was shattered, our response needed to address every aspect of their lives in a holistic way. For example, we could not begin healing the effects of trauma on the mind when people were homeless or had a limb amputated and could not look after their physical wellbeing.

From the perspective of holistic healing, we do not look at the mind's need for healing as separate from the needs of the body or the spirit. We look at the person as a human being and assess what needs must be met to support that person to receive healing. So, when we visit a rural village with our mobile medical clinic, our team consists of a doctor, paediatrician, nurses, social workers, counsellors we have trained, students and volunteers and me as Director and a psycho-therapist. We recognise that as professional health workers there are borders or boundaries to the various disciplines we bring to the clinic, and for us it is vital to our work that these boundaries are respected at the same time as we bring a holistic perspective to each person's suffering.

From the perspective of civil war, I may say that in many respects the war could be a conflict over borders, and that in the final outcome the power of the Sri Lankan State destroyed the border erected by the Tamil Tigers. This has made me reflect that if the consequence of any government achieving a borderless nation is the deaths and shattering of ordinary people's lives, doesn't that raise the question of what would it mean to be a borderless church? Our experience with the Centre for Holistic Healing (CHH) is that we don't impose divisions on the experience of a suffering person when we assess their suffering. It doesn't matter what faith they belong to, we will help them. We don't separate the mind from the body or the material from the spiritual. When we respond to their suffering holistically, we endeavour to both respect the borders or boundaries of professional knowledge, while working as cooperatively and in as an integrated manner as is needed for the circumstance of the person. This practice reflects our faith conviction that God in Christ is incarnate in human flesh, that is, body, mind and spirit are intimately inter-related even as each is a unique dimension making up the wholeness of the human person.

Our belief and practice are increasingly supported by huge breakthroughs in brain research in recent years, especially scientific developments discovering new knowledge about the effects of psychological trauma, abuse, and neglect. Research has revealed that trauma produces physiological changes such as changes to the brain's alarm system, an increase in stress hormone activity, and alterations in the brain's filtering of relevant from irrelevant information. Trauma also compromises the brain areas that communicate the physical, embodied feelings of being alive.[1] This has brought new awareness of embodied therapies into service, alongside more traditional modalities of 'talking therapies' to connect with others and deepen personal understanding, and alongside pharmacological therapies that can shut down inappropriate alarm reactions. In my own experience of recovery from PTSD, I have benefitted from anti-depressant medication. I do yoga in the mornings. While sometimes I feel sleepy and my mind wanders away, with much effort I bring back my mind to focus on yoga and I will feel much better. I also do a breathing exercise after which I can feel restored. I am rekindling my habit of playing music before going to bed. I maintain a spiritual practice of morning prayer with the open bible on my lap, reading and meditating on scripture. This helps connect me to God and to those with whom I share my faith. Recently my meditation on Psalm 91 evoked deep within me a feeling of the presence of God. So, all three modalities for trauma recovery are important to me, and we make every endeavour to instruct our trainee counsellors in the benefits of the different modalities for holistic healing.

Along with the expansion of human knowledge about illness and disease, one of the changes that a holistic perspective is bringing to the practice of healing is the creation of new communities of health practice. The Centre for Holistic Healing in Sri Lanka is a small example of the move from discipline-specific services such as medical services (hospitals, clinics, medical centres) to other sociologically-based services such the Motor Neurone Disease Association in the UK, or to multi-disciplinary services such as the Trauma Centre in the US. As with CHH, these new communities of health practice have been motivated by the experience of sufferers (or health professionals) who have felt that their experience has been overlooked or marginalised by the mainstream of health providers.

However, it would be folly for the church to think that new communities of health practice - which are often internally borderless in their holistic focus - can live without taking account of the border or boundary between their new form of health practice and the more established forms of health practice. In Sri Lanka, CHH has only recently been able to receive patients from an established psychiatric hospital for inclusion in our programs. This is an exciting and welcome development as we build trust between our organisations and explore ways to share our experience of care and healing. It is a work in progress.

While I understand that it is possible to talk about God's borderless reign, I suggest that the reality of death through war and violence also marks an all too human border that is intrinsic to the human condition and is established in God's creation. If we find it helpful to think of God as borderless, or in more traditional language, omnipotent, it is an inescapable truth of God's good creation that humankind is limited by death. Death marks a border that physically separates humankind from God. And when death comes prematurely and savagely as the result of war and violence, it is important to say that death is then an offence against God and marks humankind with the burden of injustice and sin. This is the stark reality of life today in Sri Lanka for our people and many across the nation. The stain of war and death has left a terrible burden of chaos, mistrust and unhealed wounds of grief and trauma.

We have developed vocational training programs to support war widows whose livelihood has been destroyed, and we have been able to support some orphaned children to access education and training. We assist amputees who have suffered the loss of limbs due to wounds of war to receive prosthetic limbs. We provide kindergarten and child care services to children and families whose lives have been shattered and displaced by war. All of these endeavours are the foundations on which we address the war trauma that affects peoples' mental health, including the grief of families for those who were 'disappeared' by the army or the government during the conflict, and those whose loved-ones graves were bull-dozed by the army to remove the remembrance of Tamil war dead. In the face of the spiritual reality of death which daily confronts our CHH, I am left to wonder how fruitful some of the questions this conference asks of us are. In truth, I cannot get my own mind around them while living with PTSD, let alone provide a thoughtful analysis of how better to heal the minds of those who suffer such depth of injustice and violence. I never expected that my exposure to these realities would cause my own mind and body to suffer as it has the past few years. So, I will finish my paper with a question for the conference and to CSI which is 'who heals the minds and bodies of the healers?'

I used to write poetry until my mind could no longer concentrate enough to write. I used to pray regularly until my mind was so tortured it refused to rest. So I yearn to be held in the solidarity and care of the Church of South India. I am grateful for what Christ has called me to do, and for the Spirit's gift of my ministry amongst our people. I have lived for my work – this work. But when my mind was shut down by a body too traumatised to go on working, I wondered if I had any worth. And then an overseas friend invited me to join in a journey of the spirit through Ignatian spirituality and my heart was touched by God's unconditional love that gave me my human worth. I am grateful for the support I received from overseas when I felt alone. But why did that support not come from CSI? Perhaps the borders between our Dioceses in India and the war-wearied Jaffna Diocese need to be transformed so that we are a church in solidarity with each other's wounds, and we can holistically and compassionately answer my question: 'we are called as sisters and brothers to heal the minds and bodies of all who are wounded healers?'

I trust this poem that I wrote in 2001 while the civil war was still raging, may strengthen us all to be the church that can answer my question.

The Cry of the Poor

Help of the helpless
send us helpers

Who commit themselves
and forget themselves

Who love us more
than they love themselves

Who befriend the poor
and care for the sick

Who "hate" the riches
and suffer with us

Who make the captives
mighty heroes

Who serve the slaves
and shame the masters

Who feed the hungry
and clothe the naked

Who unmask the evil
and dethrone the wicked

Who always take sides
with the oppressed

Who speak the truth
and do the just

Who thirst for justice
and "fight" for peace

Who work not for awards
and count not the cost

Who "fight" until the end
and never betray

Who serve the least, the last
and the lost.   Amen

Endnotes

[1] B. Van Der Kolk, *The Body Keeps the Score: mind, brain and body in the transformation of trauma*. Penguin Books. 2015. pp. 2-3.

12

Rethinking Ecclesia:
Eucharist at the Centre with Undefined Borders

Arul Dhas

There are different ways of understanding and comprehending Ecclesia, the Church. Nobody doubts or questions the headship of Christ in the Church. However, how do we understand the constitution and the function of the church? How do we understand the nature and mission of the church? Who are or could be members of the church? Are there any criteria? If so, what are the inclusion and exclusion criteria? These and similar questions come time and again to many who are concerned about the Church. As we celebrate Seventieth year of the ecumenical church – The Church of South India, it is very fitting that we have gone into this exercise of rethinking ecclesia.

In this paper, I would like to explore this question from healing ministry point of view. I should admit that my reflections and thoughts will be from my long association and involvement in the health dimension of the church. I would like to put forth a position where the emphasis of the church should be the centrality of Eucharist and meaning of this sacrament as its identity and fulcrum of its functioning.

This shift will facilitate us to include everyone who is touched by the brokenness of the Lord Jesus Christ in life.

1.   Healthcare Institutions

Both from the beginning and from the twenty centuries of church history we understand that health and healing have been at the top priority of the church. We understand from the threefold ministry of Lord Jesus that preaching, teaching and healing are important components of the mission. The church has therefore understood the hospitals and related establishments as the health wing of the church. When hospices began in the history of the church, they were the places of hospitality. The institution as a committed host took care of the guests who came there for help.

The relationship between the host and guest has been seen as sacred. It is seen as the demonstration of Matthew 25:36, *"I was sick, and you took care of me"*. It was seen as Mother Theresa understood, *'I see the face of Jesus in the person sitting on the streets'*. As institutions, whatever we do to the sick and the suffering is seen as something done to the Lord. Therefore, healing ministry has become not only the mandate to the church but also as the authentic and powerful witness in the world. Therefore, viewing the nature and identity of the church from the healing ministry perspective will not be a misguided route. In a way the methodology which is adopted here is trying to define something from its functions. It is different from deriving the functions of something based on the defined nature of that thing.

2.   Theological basis of healing ministry

Judeo-Christian tradition unmistakably considers God as God of health and healing. It is attested in Exodus 15:26, *"I am the Lord who heals you"*. God is the God of life, and not of death. The son of God, our Lord Jesus Christ is understood as the healer. Christ demonstrated this through the healing miracles. Throughout his ministry, Jesus healed many people. In addition to the fact that Jesus healed many, it is interesting to note that the calling of the disciples includes healing. If we summarize, God is the healer, Christ is the healer, disciples are healers and now the Church is the healer. Church is the temple of healing.

3.   An analogy of hospital

Rev. A.C. Oommen, one of the chaplains who formulated the chaplaincy ministry in Christian Medical College, Vellore gave a beautiful analogy to get clarity of the nature and identity of hospitals in Christian mission. He described hospital as a temple, doctors, nurses and others as *Poojari's* (priests), patients who come to the hospital as the devotees who come to the temple to have a darshan (view, audience) of God, fees paid by the patient are offering given to God. Those who are wounded and hurt (both emotionally and physically) come to hospital. The healthcare professionals work towards healing. Through the ministry of the healthcare professionals, the patients who are physically, emotionally and spiritually hurt receive God's healing touch. Healthcare professionals are agents of healing.

4.   Prayer, devotion and symbols

In a Christian hospital, when a patient asks for prayer, often s/he thinks of Christ. Many who walk into the hospital are aware of the history of the hospital and even the identity of the hospital. From an ecclesiastical point of view, anyone who prays and pays devotion to Christ could be considered as part of the Christian fellowship. Once I witnessed a Muslim coming very close to the pulpit in the hospital chapel and started praying *namas* (prayer) as it was his prayer time. Of course, he would have thought of God in his own way. It is worth noting that he felt comfortable to pray in the sanctuaries of a Christian chapel.

In most religions, symbols play a major role. Human beings are created in such a way that we attach meaning to different symbols which in turn give us strength to go forward. I would like to highlight few symbols which I have found in the context of healing ministry. The first one is walking around the centre of worship with devotion. It is a common sight in the hospital chapel where I work to see someone going around the altar with folded hands, sometimes even when the worship service is going on. The question is, will God be pleased with this gesture of worship? Most often, it was clear that the one who was walking around was a Hindu by religious affiliation. Because he expresses devotion to Christ, could he be referred to as a Christian also?

Another expression of people's devotion is in the form of candle lighting. Till recently, there was a candle stand in front of the hospital where I work. People from different religious backgrounds came and lighted candles as a sign of devotion and prayers to God. There was a cross at the top of it just to indicate that it is a Christian place and people who light candle normally has this feeling that they are paying devotion to Christ. Some circulate the candle as if they are doing *arthi* (holding it in the hand and moving in a circular form) in front of the candle stand. Some even fall prostrate there without worrying about who is seeing or not. Some light incense in front of the candle stand.

These practices by and large come from the Hindu religious practices. Those who perform them do in this manner since they are familiar with this tradition. It is also very clear that while they do this, they think of Christ in their mind. The prayers they offer at this point of time are offered to Christ, as they believe. The question for us now is, will Christians consider this as a Christian practice and accept them in the Christian fellowship? Will the Church accept this as a genuine expression of one's devotion to Christ?

One may also ask another question here. Simply because someone does a Christian ritual will he become a Christian? Will someone who does a religious symbol meaningfully becomes an adherent of that religion? What should constitute someone to be called a Christian externally? Here we are not talking about the internal commitment and conviction to follow Christ which requires different set of observations.

5.   Baptism and Eucharist

Two dominical sacraments are very important in protestant tradition to identify someone as a Christian. The general understanding of the Church is: One should be baptized and be a partaker in the Holy Eucharist to become a Christian. Since the Lord Jesus himself gave these two as commands they are given higher importance than other sacraments. Baptism is seen an entry into the Christian family and Eucharist as something which sustains in the faith with a mystical union with Christ, in a relational manner.

Eucharist highlights a personal identity with Christ. The central focus of this sacrament is the sacrificial love of Christ. Here again I would like to bring my experience in the context of healing ministry. Often Christians who are hospitalised look forward to take communion during their stay in the hospitals. Some do this just as a practice, which is taking communion weekly or monthly. Some do just before they go for some major procedure or surgery. Some even take communion while they feel the need of reconciliation and healing.

6.   Eucharist as a healing and inclusive experience

The sacrament of Eucharist has the mystery of suffering and pain at the centre of its meaning. The liturgy in its introduction has "On the night on which he was betrayed" as a critical introduction. The sacrament of Eucharist embodies the human experience. Particularly, the experience of betrayal, brokenness, hurt, pain and suffering are in the midst of this. Hurtful memories are transformed into memorial of thanksgiving. In the liturgy, confession plays a prelude to the breaking of the bread.

One important factor here is commonness of suffering in the context of the hospital. Most go through pain and suffering not only physically but also emotionally and spiritually. Therefore, experiencing Eucharist during hospitalisation has a special meaning – religious, spiritual and emotional. I vividly remember an incident where the patient was hesitant to receive the communion at the beginning. After an amount of time in prayer, recollection of past events and singing the patient said that he was ready to take the communion. Particularly in hospitals, holy communion is taken with lot of respect and meaning.

People are able to associate their suffering with Christ's suffering and they are able to receive hope and transformation which Christ offers. When it is taken with the family members and others, it gives an experience of healing in the local relational context too. There is also the solidarity with the church universal in the midst of a small room/place of the hospital. Eucharist gives identity, nurture and growth in the Christian faith. It gives healing and helps people to experience wholeness.

In the hospital context there have been other experiences too with regard to Eucharist. After the worship service in the hospital chapel one day an ardent devotee came and asked for holy sacraments. When asked about whether he believes in Christ, he assured that he believes in Christ and he was pleading for the sacraments. However, by religious affiliation, he was a Hindu. There are many from the Christian community and church leadership who will be upset if holy sacraments are given to him. But the man was very earnest and looked genuine. As a body of Christ, it looked very appropriate to give communion to him and welcome him into this fellowship. He felt the need for this fellowship in the context of suffering and pain. As a healing community, it is mandatory that we extend the healing touch to that man as representatives of Christ's healing community.

Therefore, the question which comes to our minds is, could ecclesia be understood as a fellowship where there are no borders. There is a centre – the experience of brokenness and hurt is the starting point of becoming a member of this fellowship. In other words, in the middle of the Christian experience is the cross of Christ. This includes the betrayal, brokenness, hurt and pain Jesus experienced. A believer is able to identify himself/herself with this experience of the Lord Jesus. At the appropriate time this experience of pain gets transformed into an experience of thanksgiving. The follower/ believer/ disciple starts to experience healing due to the Eucharist (thanksgiving).

In the middle of this transforming experience, the believer is able to find solidarity with others who go through pain and suffering, and experience healing. All those who are broken are welcome to come to this centre and experience this transformation through this Eucharistic experience. There is no definition of the borders. Probably we need to ask a question, whether we need a border at all. Closer we come to the centre, closer we come to one another. Farther we go from the centre, farther we go away from each other. Therefore, there is an invitation to come closer to this experience of transformation in the lives of the believers. Probably there is no need to define the borders. Church is the temple of healing, hospitable to all guests. At the centre of its experience is brokenness and healing demonstrated in Eucharist.

13

Affirming Alternative Archetypes of Dalits' Psyche:

A Therapeutic Ecclesiastical Response from Jungian Analytical Psychology

A. Israel David

Part I

Dalits and Borderless Church

Borders are not new to Dalits. Borders are mundane to the Dalits. These borders- the geographical, the emotional, the social, the biological, the economical, the religious, the political etc- are not strange to them. They are very much familiar both with the creators of these borders and those who thrive to sustain these borders. It is not unknown to them that these borders are forced on them during their life time and beyond. They are also accustomed to the consequences of the borders and are conscious that the 'dominant' cross over to their territory and a reversal is not permitted for the Dalits. In the realities of 'border-centred life' of Dalits, a borderless church seems to gain its significance. The paper proceeds from two hypotheses

1. There is a significant relationship between the existence of 'borders' and the 'images' in the psyches of the dominant and of Dalits.

2. The possibility of a borderless church is significantly related to the healing of psyches that result in affirming alternative archetypes.

These hypotheses are developed based on my constant struggle to understand the source of forced altered narratives of Dalits from a psychological perspective.[1] This narrative, I believe, is the result of religion-sanctioned perspectives of pollution and impurity that constantly remind the Dalits of their vulnerability and force them to live in margins and periphery.

It is my opinion that these perspectives have impacted and influenced the Dalit community psyche. Each individual Dalit is part of the community in which she/he is born. In other words, Dalits' community carried this psyche for centuries and being oppressed, discriminated, stigmatized, marginalized, untouchabl-ised and low caste-lised by the dominant for a long time. It appears that the individual psyche and behaviour cannot depart and rescue itself from these community psyche. The most bothering question that emerges is how is it possible for the community psyche to influence the individual?

It is in this context Carl Jung's analytical psychology persuade us to believe that the individual psyche of Dalits has a community dimension.

Part II

Images of Dalits: A Forced Archetype

If human behaviour, thoughts and actions are outcome and product of human's psyche, the attitude towards Dalits by the dominant is related to the psyche of both the Dalits and the dominant. The 'images of Dalits' by the Dalits and the dominant seem to be the product of the psyches of both. A brief study of Carl Jung's analytical psychology clarifies the relationship between the psyche and images. Carl Jung (1875-1961)[2], a follower of Sigmund Freud[3] and psychoanalytic tradition, established *analytic psychology* after observing several cultures of the world. He also studied the ancient mythology and Eastern Religious views. Further, he conversed with various figures, means the characters, and reported that these persons are "archetypal characters that make the collective unconscious."[4] Though there are several concepts related to Jung's analytical psychology, for the purpose of the present study the following section presents only the significant conclusions of Jung namely collective unconscious and archetype.

The Collective unconscious and Archetypes

Psyche: Jung understands Psyche in its totality which includes psychic processes, conscious and unconscious. For him psyche is self-regulating system like the body.[5] For him the "personality as whole is the psyche, the totality of all psychic processes, conscious and unconscious; it embraces all thought, feeling and behaviour and helps the individual adapt to the social and psychical environment."[6] He differed with Freud's concept of *personal unconscious* and believed in *Collective unconscious,* though he agreed with Freud in accepting that the unconscious state of psyche "consists of thoughts and images that are difficult to bring into awareness…each of us was born with this unconscious material, and it is basically the same for all people. According to Jung, just as we inherit physical characteristics, from our ancestors, we also inherit unconscious psychic characteristics."[7] It is like inheriting the instinctive of behaviours. These images are innate, universal and heredity. In other words, human mind is not blank at birth, but born with a blue print. The collective unconscious is formed by psychological inheritance, including the knowledge and experiences. [8] It can also be called as genetic learning.[9]

Archetypes: He was confidence in his conviction that the unconscious is "made up of primordial images. Jung described these images in terms of potential to respond to the world in a certain way. Thus, new-borns react so quickly to their mother because the collective unconscious holds an image of a mother for each of us…Jung referred to these images collectively as archetypes."[10] These archetypes represent universal patterns. He was firm that each archetype is significant to human typical life situations and there are limitless archetypes that "were inborn tendencies that play a role in influencing human behaviour."[11] The stereotyped processes, that is archetype, are related to 'imagery' to Jung, not related to object or interpersonal relations.[12] However, he points out four significant archetypes in his theory of human personality namely persona, anima, animus and shadow.

Persona: How do we present ourselves to the world is the persona, including the revealed and concealed real self.[13] The children behave in their respective social situations according to their persona by adapting the community's expectations and norms.

Anima and Animus: "The anima is the feminine side of the male, the animus is the masculine side of the female. According to Jung, deep inside every masculine man is a feminine counterpart. Deep inside every feminine woman is a masculine self."[14] Hence each human being holds an 'unconscious image' of man and woman and the conceptualization of man and woman is based on these images that the human beings carry for a long time from the birth, inherited from the ancestors.

Shadow: The shadow is the cause for all the behaviours that are unacceptable to the society and personal values. It is like Freud's id and animal in nature.[15] "Although the name may be bit melodramatic, the *shadow* contains the unconscious part of ourselves that is essentially negative, or to continue the metaphor, the dark side of our personalities. It is the evil side of the humankind. The shadow is located partly in the personal unconscious in the form of repressed feelings and partly in the collective unconscious. Jung pointed out that evil is personified in the myths and the stories of all cultures."[16] Shadow includes envy, greed, prejudice, hate, wildness, chaos, unknown and aggression.

The Self: Self is the central archetype that unites the personality.[17] In other words, the unifying psyche is what self is to Jung. This includes all the potential of the self. An individual can achieve a cohesive self like the self-actualization of Abraham Maslow.

Ann Hopwood argues,

> the archetypes predisposes us to approach life and to experience it in certain ways, according to patterns laid down in the psyche... These images find expression in the psyche, in behaviour and in myths. It is only archetypal images that are capable of being known and coming to consciousness, the archetypes themselves are deeply unconscious and unknowable. *[18]*

In other words, inaccessible to the conscious mind, though they are in the memory.[19]

Jung seems to believe strongly that each culture both written and oral narratives either reflect or affirm these archetypes. Moreover, he asserted that the collective unconscious and the images are found in all cultures that are usually expressed in art, folklore, and mythology. What we are and how we behave is directly related to the notions that are found in the collective unconscious. For example, the concept or the notion of women is derived from the collective unconscious of individual.[20]

The Images of Dalits and Forced Archetypes

If Carl Jung is to be believed,[21] as I do, then there is a strong probability to relate the images of Dalits to the psyche of both the Dalits and the dominant. At one hand, the question is where do a new born child of dominant caste receive their perception of the Dalits as untouchables? How are they aware of the borders that are created by their ancestors? How are the dominant able to continue to sustain the images of the Dalits? What is the source of these perceptions and images?

On the other hand, how did the Dalits believe for several centuries that they are untouchables? Is it not that the Dalits were forced to believe that they were untouchables? What forced our Dalit brothers and sisters to carry the footwears in their hands when they crossed the streets of the so-called high caste? How did these boundaries come into existence in the first place?   I conclude that the psyche in general and the collective unconscious seems to be one of the sources of these images. The borders- the geographical, the social, the biological, the economical, the religious, the political are the products of the archetypes that exist in the psyche of the people.

What are these archetypes in the psyche? The 'images of Dalits' in the psyche are the archetypes that direct the human behaviour, especially the dominant. For example, I believe, the 'untouchability' is an archetype that exists in the minds of the dominant and the Dalits for centuries, mentally inherited from their ancestors. Ambedkar uses another two significant aspects of human behaviour in relation with untouchability namely 'un-seeable' and 'un-approachable'.[22] The 'impurity' and 'pollution' are other archetypes. The borders are the external signs and symptoms of these archetypes. I believe that the Dalits are forced to live in the margins because of the archetypes such as 'impurity' and 'pollution' exist in the psyche of the dominant which have been inherited and transferred from one generation to another generation. The stigmatization, the oppression and the discrimination are, in fact, due to these archetypes. This, however, no way transfers the blame to the psyche of the ancestors of the dominant, but it demands a change in the psyche of the present generation.

Further, these archetypes are sustained for several centuries by sanction and legitimization of the religion, and political compulsions. These archetypes have been forced into the psyche of the Dalits and made them to believe what they are is natural. The wounded psyche, the broken emotions, low self-esteem and acceptance of the so-called low status for a considerable time could be based on these forced psyches. If any change is expected in the human behaviour, the human psyche needs healing. It means finding alternative archetypes of psyche is essential. Unless there is healing of psyche the Christ communities and borderless churches may not see their logical fulfilment.

Part III

Affirming the Alternative Archetype: A Therapeutic Ecclesiastical Response

Recognizing the term and the name 'Dalit' as an empowering archetype

Is it possible to create a new archetype in the psyche of the dominant and Dalits to heal the wounds? Or is there any existing 'image' of the Dalits that need to be brought to the conscious minds of both? It is this search and struggle leads one to reimagine the very name 'Dalits'[23] as an empowering archetype. People like Gangadhar Pantawane and M C Raj view the term 'Dalit' as a symbol of change which can bring a revolution. M C Raj's book entitled *Dyche-The Dalit Psyche A Science of Dalit Psychology,* is an attempt in this direction to study and show the positive natures of Dalits. Further, there is a paradigm shift in comprehending the psyche of Dalits from 'wounded and broken' to 'liberated and unbroken' psyche. M C Raj has named his current newsletter on Dalits as 'Unbroken People.'

To identify the 'untouchables,' terms like Dalits, Scheduled Castes, Harijans, Adi Dravida, Adi Karnataka, Adi Andhra are being used. In addition, James Massey adds that there are different names given for Dalits such as *"Dasa, Dasyu, Raksasa, Asura, Avarna, Nisada, Panchama, Mletcha, Svapaca, Chandala, Achuta,"*[24] which have historical roots. M E Prabhakar says that the term Dalit was first used by Maratha social reformer Jyotirao Govindrao Phule (1827-1890), also known as Mahatma Jyotirbao Phule. Phule used this term to describe the oppressed and the broken state of the outcastes and untouchables.[25] Ramachandra Kshirasagar, in his book entitled *Dalit Movements and Its Leaders (1857-1956),* notes that in 1928 a Depressed Class newspaper used the term *Dalit Bandu* to denote friends of Dalits.[26]

In addition, in 1930s the term Dalit was widely used by the Dalits as a Hindi and Marathi translation for the term 'Depressed Classes' which was used by the Simon Commission. In 1948, Ambedkar used this term in his Marathi speeches as a translation for 'broken men.' "In *the Untouchables,* published in 1948, Ambedkar chose the term 'broken men,' as an English translation of 'Dalit' to refer to the original ancestors of the Untouchables."[27] However, Ambrose Pinto in his book *Dalits In Karnataka* denies that Ambedkar used the term 'Dalit.'[28]

In early 1970s, this term was used by the Dalit activists from Mahar Community.[29] ME Prabhakar writes that especially in 1973, the Dalit Panther Movement used this term in their manifesto, inspired by their leader Namdeo Dhasal and popularized the term.[30] Gopal Guru adds that in Dalit Panthers' manifesto, the term Dalit was used "as a revolutionary category for its hermeneutic ability to recover the emancipatory potential of the historical past of Dalit culture."[31] There after the term has been used by the Dalit writers, activists, and movements to refer to the nature of oppression and the identity of the oppressed communities.[32] In April 1981, Arvind P Nirmal delivered the valedictory address, which laid the foundation for the construction of Dalit theology, entitled "Towards a Sudra Theology", at the Carey Society of United Theological College, Bangalore. Nirmal says that the discussion that preceded the address at UTC confirmed that the Sudras preferred to be called and addressed as Dalits.[33] According to Pinto, they preferred the term Dalit to harijans which was used by Gandhi, which means 'children of God.'[34]

The Term as a Symbol of Change and Revolution

There seems to be a shift in using the term 'Dalit' from the past in which it was used to denote the pathos of Dalit community. According to Daniel Premkumar, people like Gangadhar Pantawane do not consider that the term Dalit refers to the lower caste but as a 'symbol of change and revolution.'[35]

     A. Israel david

Even James Massey agrees with Gangadhar's view of the term Dalit. He says,

> This term for them (Dalits) is not a mere name or title, it has in fact, become an expression of hope for them in recovering their past identity... It must be remembered that dalit does not mean low caste, or poor, it refers to the state of a section of people to which they have been reduced and how they are in that predicament.[36]

This positive aspect of the term 'Dalit' has given a single identity to the Untouchable community in India. In India, the Dalits are not followers of a monoculture, but they are a multi-cultural community. They are multilingual and follow many religions such as Hinduism, Sikhism, Buddhism, Islam and Christianity. Despite following many cultures, religions and speaking different languages, Dalits consider themselves as one community. Abraham Ayrookuzhiel confirms this as he states that Dalits who follow different religions are attempting to come out as 'one people' to fight against the socio-economic, political and cultural marginalization.[37] For V Devasahayam, the term Dalit has been used in Dalits' search for a better life.[38]

Biblical scholars use this term 'Dalit' mainly to derive an exclusive methodology towards Dalit theology which is rooted in the incarnation of historical Jesus. However, the Dalit Theology is inclusive in its approach and it believes in liberation of all communities. Initially Dalit theology viewed Dalits as children of God like the chosen Jews, but now Dalit theology associates the term 'Dalit' as agents of change'. James Massey has exclusively used the term as a Perspective to bring out Biblical commentaries on Dalits. In addition, there are attempts by people like M C Raj to bring out the positive natures of Dalits by using the term. The term 'Dalit' also has motivated many Dalit communities and leaders to provide leadership within the church and outside the church. Their struggles to achieve justice have been motivated by the identity 'Dalit' and it has motivated them even to appeal to United Nations and in International Conferences such as Durban Conference in South Africa.

The present paper proceeds from this vantage point that the very term Dalit itself is a positive motivation to the community in their journey towards liberation. A borderless church will be possible through the recognition of the paradigm shift which is happening in the psyche of the Dalits. They are not just controlled by their pain and pathos but a positive psyche that can create other new archetypes such as Dalits as actualizing community, empowered community, touchable community, see able community, approachable community, and fully functioning community that will resist the 'created opinions and images' of the dominant. These new archetypes will naturally lead to new just social orders such as Christ communities, borderless church and reign of God.

A Therapeutic Ecclesiastical Response

Can the church ignore such a great paradigm shift in understanding the status of the Dalits? The ecclesia with its new call to be a borderless church can be a healing agent if it engages in deconstructing, demasking and reconstructing the oppressive archetypes or the images of the Dalits. These archetypes have been internalized by the Dalits to believe 'what they are'. Dalits have been experiencing the forced internalized stories about their social status for centuries, even though they naturally possess high values. Dalits were continuously forced to overlook their natural and nurtured values because of the dominant internalized stories. The deconstruction as a process can deconstruct people in these identity stories, which are constituted and constructed by the dominant cultures. According to Michel Focault[39], the dominant stories are imposed from outside to interpret and to give meaning to one's events, hence they cannot be authentic. They cannot bring meaning to one's living experiences. But the meaning which is attributed by a person to events will determine the behaviour. This outside story, as it is noted earlier, is from a dominant culture of a society, which is oppressive, because it tries to give meaning to the life-events of the people. A community is forced to internalize the 'truths and relationship' from outside. These 'truths' from outside are 'limiting, disqualifying, and oppressive,' and determine 'who people are', and 'what people ought to be.' The patterns of life style are shaped by these truths. In this process, the old stories will be demasked, and 'unmasked.' Dalits will narrate the problems, based on the old internalized story, focusing on how these problems have an impact on their understanding of their self-relationships.

Thus, the deconstruction helps Dalits to 'unpack their stories' which would lead them to visualize the way the construction of their stories has taken place in their larger social contexts and systems. The purpose of this process is to 'deconstruct problematic narratives.' Especially the belief systems, attitudes, feelings and practices will be brought out. As there are values, beliefs, and lifestyles that are forced upon the psyches of Dalits, they were made to believe that these are the truths about them. The church should provide space for Dalits to 'de-mask' and 'unpack.'

Further, the Dalit theology could provide the theological framework to the ministry of the church in its attempt to recognize the name 'Dalit' as powerful tool to create a borderless church. Dalit theology brings out the brighter side of the contexts of the Dalits to the fore such as the possibilities of the hope and transformation to the living contexts of the Dalits. Massey points out that the 'slave nation' is transformed and liberated in to a 'nation' by God. In other words, once they were considered as 'no-people' and now as 'people.' Massey further uses the expression of 'solidarity' in Dalit theology to re-discover the message of hope based on praxis.[40] In a sense the Dalit theology confirms the presence of virtues and values like solidarity and hope in Dalit community. Dalits have become the agents of this positivity and hope.

The pulpit should become a powerful tool and provide space for the deconstruction, reconstruction and demasking of these internalized stories that emerge from the psyche. Further, the pulpit is a tool to affirm the term 'Dalit' as a empowering archetype.

Concluding Words

A rethinking of ecclesia includes recognition of the term 'Dalit' as an alternative archetype that results in healing of psyches. Healing of psyches are integral part of Christ communities that can affirm the process towards a borderless church. A borderless church will be 'Dalit' centred congregations, means presence of positivity, hope, justice, equality, peace, companionship, and will recognize the Dalits as 'pastoral community' that is an honest and respectful companion to 'others' including the dominant to experience health. Hence the therapeutic ecclesiastical response is an attempt to bring the name 'Dalit,' a sign of divine aspects, to the consciousness of the communities. Borders are not new to the Dalits and healing of these borders are also not new to them. There is hope.

Endnotes

[1] Please refer my article in the Bangalore Theological Forum in its issue Vol. XLVIII, NO. 1 June 2016, titled Deconstructing altered and reconstructing alternative narratives of the marginalized: Reaffirming the innate empowerment through pastoral counselling".

[2] "Jung was born in 1875 in Kesswil, a small town in Switzerland. He was highly introspective child who kept to himself, largely because he felt no one would understand the inner experiences and thoughts with which he was preoccupied. Jung spent many childhood hours pondering the meaning of the dreams and supernatural visions he experienced...Jung's desire to understand himself led him to the young field of psychiatry. He earned his medical degree from the University of Basel in 1900, and went to Zurich to study with Eugen Bleuler, a leading authority on schizophrenia. Later he worked in Paris with Pierre Janet, who was conducting pioneering work on consciousness and hypnosis. Naturally, Jung's curiosity about the human mind soon brought him into contact with Freud's work." Jerry M. Burger, *Personality*, sixth edition, (Australia: Thomson Wadsworth, 2004), 108-109.

³ Freud is the father of psychanalytic tradition of psychology who did topography of the human mind. He believed human psyche consists of conscious, sub conscious and unconscious states. And in unconscious there are conflicts between id, ego and super ego. He further trusted that human behaviour is determined and the two instincts namely thanatos and libido controls human behaviour.

⁴ Jerry M. Burger, *Personality,* sixth edition, (Australia: Thomson Wadsworth, 2004), 108-109.

⁵ For detailed study of psyche by Jung refer Carl Jung, *On the Nature of the Psyche,* Translated by R F C Hull, (London: Routledge Classics, 2012), 79-171

⁶ Richard D. Gross, *Psychology -The Science of Mind and Behaviour,* 2ⁿᵈ ed. (London: Hodder and Stoughton, 1992), 921.

⁷ Jerry M. Burger, *Personality,* sixth edition, (Australia: Thomson Wadsworth, 2004), 106. For further reading on the contrasts between Freud and Jung refer C G Jung, *Modern Man in Search of Soul,* translated by W. S. Dell and Cary F. Baynes, (New York: Harcourt, Brace and Company, 1933), 132-142.

⁸ "What are the Jungian Archetypes? The 4 major Jungian Archetypes", Kendra Cherry, in *personality Psychology,* https://verywellmind.com accessed on 22ⁿᵈ August 2018.

⁹ "The structure and dynamics of the psyche" by C. G. Jung (Vol. 8 of Collected works) Translated by R. F. C. hull, (London: Routledge and Kegan Paul, 1960), 588 in *Journal of Mental Science,* Vol. 108, Issue 452, January 1962, 114-115.

¹⁰ "Among many archetypes Jung described were mother, father, the wise old man, the sun, the moon, the hero, God, and death." Jerry M. Burger, *Personality,* sixth edition, (Australia: Thomson Wadsworth, 2004), 106-107.

¹¹ "What are the Jungian Archetypes? The 4 major Jungian Archetypes", Kendra Cherry, in *personality Psychology,* https://verywellmind.com accessed on 22ⁿᵈ August 2018.

¹² Ray Colledge, *Mastering Counselling Theory,* (New York: Palgrave Macmillan, 2002), 44

¹³ Richard D. Gross, *Psychology -The Science of Mind and Behaviour,* 2ⁿᵈ ed. (London: Hodder and Stoughton, 1992), 923.

¹⁴ Jerry M. Burger, *Personality,* sixth edition, (Australia: Thomson Wadsworth, 2004), 109.

[15] Richard D. Gross, *Psychology -The Science of Mind and Behaviour,* 2nd ed. (London: Hodder and Stoughton, 1992), 924.

[16] Jerry M. Burger, *Personality,* sixth edition, (Australia: Thomson Wadsworth, 2004),109.

[17] Richard D. Gross, *Psychology -The Science of Mind and Behaviour,* 2nd ed. (London: Hodder and Stoughton, 1992), 924.

[18] Ann Hopwood, "Jung's model of the psyche."

[19] J P Das, *The Working Mind,* (New Delhi: The Sage Publications, 1998), 158

[20] Refer Carl G Jung, *Four Archetypes* (Translated by R F C Hull), (London: Routledge & Kegan Paul, 2012) and "What are the Jungian Archetypes? The 4 major Jungian Archetypes", Kendra Cherry, in *personality Psychology,* https://verywellmind.com accessed on 22nd August 2018.

[21] "one criticism sometimes directed at Jung's ideas is that his theory is difficult to examine with scientific search. However, Jung did not create his ideas out of sheer fantasy. Rather, through a lifelong study of modern and ancient cultures, and through his career as psychotherapist, Jung arrived at what was for him indisputable evidence for the collective unconscious and the other constructs in this theory…Jung examined mythology, cultural symbols, dreams, and the statements of schizophrenics." Jerry M. Burger, *Personality,* sixth edition, (Australia: Thomson Wadsworth, 2004), 109.

[22] From 1935, Untouchables are also described as Scheduled Castes through the Government of India Act 1935. Ambedkar, "From Millions to Fractions," in *Dr. Babasaheb Ambedkar- Writings and Speeches,* vol. 5 *compiled* by Vasant Moon (Bombay: The Education Department of Maharastra, 1989), 229, 242, 245. For Ambedkar, untouchability has to be understood in a notional sense i.e. a person is an Untouchable because he/she belongs to an untouchable community or class. Ambedkar, "Untouchability," in *The Essential writings of B R Ambedkar,* edited by Valerian Rodrigues (New Delhi: Oxford University Press, 2002), 97. Ambedkar, "Who were the Shudras?," in *Dr. Babasaheb Ambedkar- Writings and Speeches,* vol. 7 compiled by Vasant Moon (Bombay: The Education Department of Maharastra, 1990), 114.

[23] James Massey says that the term Dalit has its root in the Sanskrit word *dal.* According to Massey, *dal* means "to crack, open, split... When used as a noun or adjective, it means burst, split, broken or torn asunder, downtrodden, scattered, crushed, destroyed, etc." James Massey, "Historical Roots," in *Indigenous…,* op. cit., 6. James Massey further explains that the Sanskrit term Dalit has a historical root to Hebrew word *dall* which means the following:To hang down, to be languid, be weakened, be low, and be

feeble…In the Bible it has been used more often as objective in order to denote the state of certain groups of people. Its basic adjective form is *dal*, masculine plural is *dalem*, and feminine, plural *dalot*, feminine singular is *dalah*. As an adjective it has been translated commonly in English as low, weak or poor. James Massey, *Towards Dalit Hermeneutics* (New Delhi: Centre for Dalit Studies, 2001), 1-4. For A P Nirmal the term Dalit means 1) the broken, the torn, the rent, the burst, the split, 2) the opened, the expended, 3) the bisected, 4) the driven asunder, the dispersed, 5) the downtrodden, the crushed, the destroyed, 6) the manifested, the displayed. A P Nirmal, "Doing Theology from a Dalits' perspective," in *A Reader in Dalit Theology* edited by Arvind Nirmal (Madras: Gurukul Lutheran Theological College and Research Institute, ND), 139.

[24] James Massey, "Historical Roots," in *Indigenous People: Dalits-Dalit Issues in Today's Theological Debate,* edited by James Massey (Delhi: ISPCK, 1994), 7

[25] M E Prabhakar, "The Search for a Dalit Theology," in *Towards a Dalit Theology* edited by M E Prabhakar (Delhi: ISPCK, 1988), 36.

[26] Ramachandra Kshirasagara, *Dalit Movements and Its Leaders 1857-1956* (New Delhi: M D Publications, 1994), 308.

[27] John C B Webster, "Who is a Dalit?" in *Dalits in Modern India-Vision and Values,* 2nd edition, edited by S M Michael (Los Angeles: Sage Publications, 2007), 76.

[28] Ambrose Pinto, *Dalits in Karnataka-In search of Identity and Equality* (New Delhi: Manak Publications Pvt Ltd. 2013), 37.

[29] Oliver Mendelsohn and Marika Vicziany, *The Untouchables-Subordination, Poverty and the State in Modern India* (New Delhi: Foundation Books, 2000), 3-4.

[30] M E Prabhakar, *The Search for a Dalit Theology…,* op. cit., 36.

[31] Gopal Guru, "The Politics of Naming," in *Seminar,* November 1998, 471.

[32] John C B Webster, *Who is a Dalit…,* op. cit., 76.

[33] Arvind P Nirmal, "A Dialogue with the Dalit Literature" in *Towards a Dalit Theology* edited by M E Prabhakar (Delhi: ISPCK, 1988), 66.

[34] Ambrose Pinto, *Dalits in Karnataka…,* op. cit., 38.

[35] Daniel Premkumar in Introductory page in *Bible and Dalit Bahujans: The Word as Fountainhead of Liberation* (Chennai: Synod Deaprtment of Dalit and Adivasi Concerns, 2003)

[36] James Massey, "Historical Roots" in *Indigenous…,* op. cit., 6-7

[37] Abraham Ayrookuzhiel, *Essays on Dalits, religion and Liberation* (Bangalore: CISRS, 2006), 108

[38] V Devasahayam, *Pollution, Poverty, and Powerlessness...*, op. cit., 1.

[39] Michel Foucault (1926–1984) was a French historian and philosopher, associated with the structuralist and post-structuralist movements. He has had strong influence not only (or even primarily) in philosophy but also in a wide range of humanistic and social scientific disciplines.

[40] James Massey, "Vision and Role of Dalit Theology,"..., op. cit., 72-73.

14

Indian Secularism and Religious Tolerance:

Challenges and Possibilities in Interfaith Harmony and Crossing boarders

Oliver Densingh

India is both a multi-religious and a secular country. It continues to be the largest democracy in the world. India from the time immemorial has been viewed as a land of hospitable, composite culture and Indian culture has immense diversity in lifestyle, religion, tradition, language, habits and much more. But in recent decades, questions have been raised and events have suggested that Indian secularism is in a crisis and its democracy is in danger. Religious fanaticism and fundamentalism which are mushrooming every day raises these questions and concerns. We are rethinking ecclesia in the context of cultural nationalism & homogenisation and identity politics in the name of unity. How does Indian version of secularism envisage a pluralistic and harmonious living together?

Origin of Secularism in the West

The term "secular" was derived from the Latin word *saeculum* which originally meant "an age or generation, the times or the world," connected with the affairs of the world, not spiritual or sacred. For Charles Taylor, the word "secular" itself is a Christian term and one can find its original meaning in a Christian context. For him, "*saeculum,* the ordinary Latin word for country or age, took on a special meaning as applied to profane time, the time of ordinary historical succession, which the human race lives through between the Fall and the Parousia."[1] In Europe, the process of secularization of the society started right from the fifteenth century Renaissance [2] and French Enlightenment which exposed the revival of the pagan Greco-Roman classicism and the opening of a new horizon of humanism contrary to the other-worldliness of the Church.[3] Classical liberalism played a pioneering role in laying the philosophical-political foundation of secularism in Europe to fight against its dogmatic past.[4] The history of the Enlightenment marked its beginning from Rene Descartes (1596-1650), [5] when he questioned the very existence of this world. His philosophical preposition "cogito ergo sum" that means "*I think; therefore, I exist,*" changed the understanding of the "self" and assisted the process of secularization.

The word "secular" and "secularization" emerged and came into use in European language about 1640s, where it was used to describe the transfer of territories previously held under the ecclesiastical control to the domination of lay political authorities.[6] During the time of scientific revolution in Europe in 16th and 17th century, secular science created the sacred or spiritual as an other-worldly domain fully separated from this-worldly realms of nature and society.[7]

As the Enlightenment saw religion as a threat to freedom, progress and modernity hence, Enlightenment rationalism became the forerunner of secularization of the Western society. The Scientific Revolution of the 16th 17th centuries changed the way educated people looked at the world. Secularism in Europe has its own history of separating the religion from civic life with the help of the process of modernization, whereas, in the context of Indian freedom struggle, it emerged to cope up with the challenge and tension of a multi-religious situation.

Therefore, by nature, the notion of secularism is not a stable one or a fixed universal category. But, according to its historical and religious context it is changing. Western secularism differs from Indian secularism in nature and in meaning.

The origin of secularism has its unique background in India

India adopted the notion of secularism from the West, which is a new phenomenon in modern history. Though the concept of secularism was imported from the West to India, the difference between Western and Indian forms of secularism is that while the former was born in the context of rationalism and domination of one religion, the latter was stimulated in the context religious tolerance and of modernizing colonial India. India adopted the idea of secularism in the context of colonialism, partition of India and in the formation of the newly formed Indian nation. To sustain religious harmony in the religious pluralistic context, national leaders adopted the idea of secularism with a lot of changes. Because of the diversity of traditions, heritage, religious practices and mutual hostility of Hindus-Muslims and Sikhs, it was no smooth passage of life in the process of secularization of India. However, the beauty of the Indian mode of secularism is that it never demanded or advocated a separation of State and religion. Indian secularism in politics was adopted voluntarily by the Indian National Congress to cope up with the multi-religious situation because, it had representatives and leaders from multi-religious and cultural background. Unlike in Europe, secularism in India arose not so much in the context of conflict with organized religion, but as an attempt to unify the followers of different religious faiths in their struggle against the British by making it the premise of a united free India.[8] Mukul

Kesavan views that the Indian National Congress from its inception was "a sort of political Nova's Ark which sought to keep every species of Indian on board."[9] However, this unity in plurality did not last long in Congress. In fact, Mahatma Gandhi wanted religion to contribute morally to politics as religion is morality. He contextualized and understood secularism as *sarva dharma samabhāva* and interpreted it as equality and toleration of all religions. But Jawaharlal Nehru wanted to keep religion away from politics. He advocated for a strong socialist democracy for India, and his concept of secularism was based on equality of every person in the social and political realm. It meant, honoring all religions equally and giving them an equal opportunity for expression. A secular State for him was a State, which protects all religions but does not favor one at the expense of the other.

Thus, right from the beginning, the Congress emphasized on multi-religiousness of Indian society, and was sensitive towards religious tolerance.[10] For the Congress, being secular meant accommodating different types of Indians equally in its fold. Secularism in this context was a way of being comprehensively nationalist.

Indian Way of Inter-religious relationship

Historically, equal treatment of religions has been the popular ethos of Indian tradition. Theistic and atheistic religious traditions lived together; Buddhism and Jainism had the opportunity to spread their anti-Vedic doctrine and views. The Chārvāka materialistic philosophy vehemently opposed Vedic ritualistic Hinduism. Amartya Sen argues that the long history of heterodoxy in India has had a bearing not only on the development and survival of democracy; it has also richly contributed to the emergence of secularism. In history, the tolerance of religious diversity is reflected in India as a shared home for Hindus, Buddhists, Jains, Jews, Christians, Muslims, Parsis, Sikhs, Bahais, and others.[11] Rulers like Ashoka promoted religious tolerance and Akbar the Great stood for the amalgamation of various religions and encouraged the promotion of different religions in the country. Akbar founded a new religious order called *Din-illahi*.[12] This order encouraged the principles of non-violence, religious tolerance and equal respect to all religions and proposed the secular value of co-existence.

Sufism which emerged from the Islamic tradition adapted devotional music and dance, and strove to establish human's communion with God, which is very much linked to the *bhakti* tradition of *bhajan* and *kirtan*. Poets like Kabir and Nayak borrowed ideas from Hindu *bhakti* tradition and Sufism. This was indeed a significant marker of India's composite culture and heritage.[13] Secularism in India, was thus, based on the pluralistic and syncretic character of society. Followers of all faiths and denominations are even now free to pursue their religious or cultural practices and the State would not discriminate against or in favour of any of them. For many Indians, *sarva dharma sambhāva*, that is, equal respect for all religions is the guiding principle of our country's secular ethos.[14] The Vedic dictum *Ekam sat vipra bahudha vadanti* (Truth is one, the wise call it differently) is the unifying factor of Indian culture.[15] Indian society is not a secular society but it became a secular State in a political sense.

Theology of religions in India has taken the realities of Asian societies, culture and religious traditions in its theologizing. For example, a sense of boundless mystery of God embedded in Asian religions and mystical tradition has been taken very seriously in Asian theology and theology of religions. Generally, in Asian theology God is not pre-defined to be known as an object but a mystery that is to be discovered by awakening of the self to God's presence within and outside and through an inward journey of mindfulness. This framework inspired the Asian theologians not to follow paths of exclusion but of integration and inter-faith relation.[16] This sense of mystery also leads one to a spirit of pluralism. Asian theology of religions echoes this diversity and value the spirit of pluralism as a joyful celebration, and not simply as a fact to be grappled with. It also resists tendencies of uniformity and homogenization. This realization has led us to view the diversity of perspectives not as a hindrance but as a great enrichment to the life of faith and religious harmony.[17]

Secularism in India after Independence

After the partition, secularism became an inevitable basis of the polity to provide security to the masses.[18] Particularly after the partition, secularism was not only the political doctrine but a social one of revolutionary character which embraced all religions and all communities in India. The painful experience of the partition of Indian Sub-Continent and the subsequent development of Hindu- Muslim conflict and hostility necessitated leaders like Gandhi and Nehru to come to a consensus to adopt a distinctive form of secularism for country's modern democratic polity. Gandhi and Nehru preferred to keep India secular in the sense that the State will not interfere with religion, though people of India will be free both in an individual and corporate sense to follow any religion of their birth or adoption.

Constitutional Secularism

Secularism in India helps the State to adopt an attitude of neutrality and impartiality towards all religions. It keeps away religion from the State affairs but values the need of religion in the society. Under the leadership of Nehru, India declared thus its policy of secularism, wherein the State would stay aloof from taking sides in religious matters. The Preamble of the Constitution clearly states that India is a "SOVEREIGN SOCIALIST SECULAR DEMOCRATIC REPUBLIC" country. However, it was only in 1976, the then Prime Minister of India Indira Gandhi, by an amendment, passed by the parliament, introduced the word "secular" into the Preamble of the Indian Constitution.[19]

The Constitution of India affirms the right to freedom of religion to all its citizens. Article 25 gives this promise, and the clause (1) says:

Subject to public order, morality and health and to the other provisions of this part, all persons are equally entitled to freedom of conscience and the right freely to profess, practice and propagate religion.[20]

The word Secularism in not there in Constitution, but the spirit of secularism and freedom of religion are explicit in the Constitution of India.

Cultural Homogenization Verses Plural Democracy: Challenges in Crossing boarders

Indian culture is a composite culture and cultural homogenization was never attempted until the recent past. Hindu fundamentalist groups like Arya Samaj,[21] Hindu Mahasaba,[22] Rashtrya Swayam Sevak,[23] Vishwa Hindu Parishad[24] and Shiva Sena[25] together constituted as the so-called Hindutva (cultural nationalism) poses a threat to the Indian secular fabric and challenges its secular Constitution. Dayananda Saraswati tried to "semitise" Hinduism, and V.D. Savarkar tried to define Hindutva as the exclusive culture of Hinduism. Thus, the fundamentalists give more importance to ideologies rather than the fundamentals of their sacred text. The Hindu fundamentalist depends on the ideologies of Savarkar's Hindutva and the writings of Golwalkar's book *Bunch of Thoughts* for their inspiration and motivation.[26]

The Hindu fundamentalist views "Hinduism" to be the true expression of secularism and considers the secularism of the Congress and other parties and movements to be pseudo-secularism or false secularism. the idea of democracy is interpreted in terms of majoritarianism and Indian nationalism is projected as Hindutva and Indian culture as Hindu culture.[27] Majority communalism is of course more aggressive, but one should not try to minimize the dangers of minority communalism either. Majority communalism feeds on minority communalism and vice-versa, thus both strengthen each other.

To quote an example, on the sixty sixth Republic day, 26 January 2015 the Indian government published an advertisement in which the words 'secular' and 'socialist' were missing from the Preamble of the

Indian Constitution. One of the Shiv Sena party leaders, Sanjay Raut said that most Indians wanted to remove these words permanently from the Constitution as India belongs to Hindus. The party also said that the word 'secular' was not relevant for the country as India is a 'Hindu Rashtra' and people of other religions can live but the Hindus will dominate. These kind of hate politics with the fascist tendency is increasing in the recent decades through right-wing parties like Rashtriya Swayamsevak Sangh.[28]

The critics of Hindutva were being targeted. The brutal killing of liberals and rational thinkers like M.M. Kalburgi and Gauri Lankesh are the recent examples. Further, sedation charges against students like Kanhaiya Kumar, the Jawaharlal Nehru University student union leader and the subsequent arrest on February 2016 shows how the colonial legislation is being used the BJP government with impunity.[29] People from Muslim and Dalit community are the major victims of the *Gau Rakshak* lynching. On 28th September 2015 the *Sangh Parivar* people killed Mohammad Akhlaq of Dadri, Uttar Pradesh on the suspicion of storing and eating beef. On 29th June 2017 a mob killed Asgar Ansari, a Muslim trader in Jharkhand, for allegedly carrying beef in his car and the event continues.[30]

Today, it poses four basic problems: territorializing of religion or territorial grounding of religion; the religious polarization and divisiveness caused by communalism invading politics; homogenization which erodes the identity of minorities and of life styles; and regeneration of their power and position within society and culture. This monoculturalism poses the utmost threat to a multicultural society like India.[31] Hindutva emphasizes that people of other faiths in India should return to Hinduism, and the love for the Motherland or *rashtra dharma* is considered as the highest value of *dharma*. Thus, RSS' aim is 'political domination through cultural homogenization.'[32]

Today, secular historiography is also being changed into communal history which imposes saffronization in education, and the Constitution which guarantees secularism is under the threat of revision. On the other side, the debates on Uniform Civil Code,[33] special provision to Kashmir in Article 370 and the minority right issues stimulate further discussion in the context of secularism. Supreme Court Judgment on Hindutva - It is also important to note that, the Supreme Court erred in concluding that Hindutva constitutes "a way of life" of the people of the subcontinent and is not to be equated with or understood as religious Hindu fundamentalism. Soon after the judgment, the RSS journal *Organiser's* article "Cultural nationalism wins over pseudo-secularism" stated that the court has fully and unambiguously endorsed the concept of Hindutva which the BJP has been propounding since its inception.[34]

History, Historiography and Saffron Education and Media

The distorted view of India's history is a major component of the saffron education. Thus, the manipulation and twist of textbooks on history, giving the Indian history a Hindu-oriented twist were revitalized. [35] Many school text books were packed with Hindu mythology, and they openly preached the glories of India's Hindu past disproportionate to reality. Such historiography will lead to the destruction of the social sciences in India.[36] What is happening to UGC and The National Council of Educational Research and Training (NCERT) is an attempt to saffronize education.

The first aim of Vidya Bharti schools (Run by RSS wing) is to develop a National System of Education which would help to build a generation of young men and women that is committed to Hindutva and infused with patriotism (Cultural Nationalisn).[37] If this is so, the question remains whether its aim enriches pluralistic society or not? Will it give space for minorities to keep their identity? This kind of education will create a communal mindset in the school children which will affect their future as well as social and inter-faith religious harmony. The same agenda continues by using media also.

For example, from 1985-1989, the Government television network, Doordharshan telecasted the great Hindu epics and religious mythological serials, the Rāmāyaṇa, Mahābhāratha, Sri Kṛṣṇa and Chanakya. These programs were inscribed with national integration themes and did hegemonic work for the nation-state.[38] Arvind Rajagopal in his book, *Politics after Television: Hindu Nationalism and the Reshaping of the Public in India* explains how these serials created a Hindutva consciousness and shaped in the minds of Hindus a Utopia of the Rama Rajya of the past and a glorious future for Hindus.

The Freedom of Religion/ Common/Uniform Civil Code

Introduction of the Uniform Civil Code and the removal of Article 370 of the Constitution that binds the State of Jammu & Kashmir into the Indian Union is another major agenda of Hindu communal politics of cultural homogenization. For example, in 1978, the Shah Bano case brought the secularism debate along with a demand for uniform civil code in India to the forefront.

It is true that every religion has a segment of conservatives over against reformists and moderates. This must be addressed as a dangerous element for religious tolerance and peacemaking. Preferably and logically in a plural and democratic secular society like India, there should be a Uniform Civil Code for all its citizens just as there is a uniform penal code. But the proposal should come from the religions, when they are ready. The beneficiary should not undermine the importance of the nation over against their religious norms. But the Uniform Civil Code cannot be achieved either through politicizing the issue or polarizing the communities.[39] The present form of cultural homogenization which is rooted in politicized Hinduism & has institutionalized caste system intrinsically. This inherent inequality cannot be the base for uniformity and equality. At the same time, religious communities should be aware of the gender inequality and human right violations that are embedded in the personal laws, and they should come forward to revisit and revise it in the light of modern democratic principles.

Current Debate

Though these debates are heavily polarized for some time, one thing to be noticed is that the opponents as well as the supporters of secularism in India are equally concerned with the rise of religious fundamentalism and fanaticism and the equality of the minorities in India. On the other hand, nobody wants to relegate religion into private sphere as in the European versions of secularism. Most of the scholars are trying to visualize a principle of tolerance, either in the traditional way or with the modern democratic principles.

For Ashis Nandi secularism an "imported idea from the Europe into South Asia" is "increasingly incompatible" in South Asian culture. Secularism was a product of the Enlightenment and modernity and this modernization causes religion-as-ideology and then makes secularism to meet its challenges to the ideology of "modern statecraft."[40] He holds that the State system in South Asia must learn something about religious tolerance from every day Hinduism, Islam, Buddhism, and Sikhism rather than wishing that ordinary believers of faiths will learn tolerance from the various fashionable secular theories of statecraft. But how far it is possible in a pluralistic context has not been explained sufficiently. For T.N. Madan, secularism is an outcome of an interaction between Protestantism and science and by nature it is incapable of countering religious fundamentalism and fanaticism.[41] Further to preserve harmony in society, Madan offers two recommendations. One is to keep religion in public life and use its resources of tolerance to prevent fanaticism and inter-religious conflicts and the other is to deconstruct the existing idea of secularism and admit the need of some form of secularism reconstructed in the Indian cultural context. In this process, education which includes history of secularism, comparative religion and inter-religious program would help largely to bring about a relevant understanding.

While Nandy and Madan demand the recovery of traditional tolerance, Chatterjee and Bhargava come close in upholding the democratic principles in their debate. Rajeev Bhargava feels that deploying the resources of religious tolerance to isolate bigotry and encourage internal reform is one of the best ways. Bhargava appreciates Indian secularism for its contextual features and believes that Indian secularism not only makes attempts to separate religion from politics but also tries to pursue the agenda of socio-religious reforms through the judiciary.

Neera Chandhoke views that secularism in India was designed to allow people to live together in civility, which the contemporary critics and opponents of secularism seem to forget.[42] In her book *Beyond Secularism: The Rights of Religious Minorities*, Chandhoke seeks to offer a framework of tolerance that is able to include respect for the minority. It was designed in India so as to regulate the devastating religious conflict, and to reassure the minorities of their safety and the domination of one religion. Hence, secularism in India was intended to allow people to live together in civility, which the contemporary critics and opponents of secularism seem to forget.[43]

She is of the opinion that equal treatment of the un-equals reproduces inequality. Interestingly, she says, secularism in contemporary India can be understood as a form of integration to the rule of majority. This is exactly so, because it is rooted in the principle of equality that is *sarva dharma samabhāva*, which requires formal respect for all religions. Such a kind of equality generates a sort of neutrality of the State towards religion, which is not enough to defend those minorities endangered by assimilation. So, if unequal people are treated equally, it will reproduces inequality.[44]

Therefore, she advocates to move from the formal equality to a "substantive equality," from equalitarianism to egalitarianism.[45] This model of "substantive equality" demands that we recognize the existence of institutionalized inequality in the society and employ helpful measures to institute tangible equality.[46] Amartya Sen has cautioned the people not to reject secularism but demand for a balanced treatment of all religious communities by the State as the preservation of religious freedom, not any way violating the principles of secularism.

Charles Taylor held that "secularism in some form is a necessity for the democratic life of religiously diverse societies."[47] In the same way, I thinks that the non-politicized Indian version of secularism and inter-faith relationship could go hand in hand to generate and uphold a harmonious living together, if confusions could be clarified with religious tolerance. Hence separation of religion and politics may not be the best solution for any problem. Presently, the West is experiencing a post-secular notion where religion has continued to impact the society (though some times in a destructive way), where religious pluralism or multiculturalism is becoming the day to day reality.

Dialogue and Peace

Hans Kung opines that, *"there can be no peace among the nations without peace among the religions," and "there can be no world peace without religious peace."*[48] Felix Wilfred, an Indian Christian theologian views that today inter-religious dialogue is an ethical imperative. Religion that cares for the well being of the society cannot fail to realize the importance of inter-religious relations. He feels that the religious traditions of India need to meet each other, and dialogue and this discourse will be part of the political and democratic process with a lot of ethical implications. A fruitful dialogue on this plane would call for a systematic self-critical activity by every religious group. When religion do not meet at the political level, the consequence is that they try to fight out each other and vanish one another in the most inappropriate of ways, jeopardizing the democratic process. Through inter-religious dialogue religious groups come to a fresh realization of what religion really is and what moral accountability it bears towards the larger society.[49]

T. K. Oommen observes that in a multi-religious context such as India, secularism can only mean religious pluralism; a societal situation in which religious groups interact with mutual respect, enter into critical dialogue and creative confrontations so as to shape a just and humane society. Therefore, secularism cannot and will not displace religion; the two will co-exist.[50]

Indian Secularism and Inter-Faith Relations: Possible ways of crossing Borders

Most of the critical study on secularism positively affirm that evoking religious tolerance either from the religious traditions or with the help of democratic principle would be the better option for harmonious living together.

Rationalizing the Social Laws of Religions with Secular Democratic Principles

One cannot undervalue the role of democratic principles in the development of post-independent India and its influence in all spheres of life. These principles promote freedom of religion and control inter-religious and intra-religious domination. Religion can build up unity among people hailing from distinct background if it allows itself for the reformation in the light of justice, freedom and equality. Religious reforms are not new to Indian context. For example, Raja Rammohan Roy's fight against socio-religious injustices and evils like *sati*, child marriage, female infanticide and untouchability were largely influenced by secular democratic principles

Though we are living in a modern world, religion and religious fundamentalism still dominate and control even intra-religious freedom of the individual. For example, till today we are debating on women entering certain religious places like Sabarimala Temple in Kerala or the Shani Shingnapur Temple, Ahmednagar. On 1 June, 2016 about 50,000 men and women signed a petition seeking a ban on triple *talaq* and the misuse of oral *talaq*. The women's rights group claims that 92 per cent Muslim women are against triple *talaq* and want it to be abolished.[51] On 22 August, 2017, the Supreme Court banned this controversial divorce practice of instant triple *talaq*. The opponents feel that this ban will start an erosion of their religious rights.[52] However, these are events which portray the orthodoxy, patriarchy and hierarchy that dominate religions even in the twenty first century. So, in a secular country like India, religions need to revise their traditional dogmas in the light of the modern value system. In this context of intra-religious domination, secular principles and the fundamental rights of the Constitution comes as a help to establish liberty, equality, justice and individual dignity.

Commitment to Secular Pluralistic Fraternity

The values expressed in the Preamble are sovereignty, socialism, secularism, democracy, justice, liberty, equality, fraternity, human dignity and the unity and integrity of the Nation. All these values carry paramount importance, but the researcher would like to highlight the value of fraternity and the unity and integrity of the nation which are much needed as values today, but less included in the political discourses. Fraternity stands for the spirit of common brotherhood/ sisterhood. In the absence of that, a plural society like India stands divided. Article-51 A (e) declares it as a fundamental duty of every citizen of India to promote harmony and the spirit of common brotherhood amongst all the people of India transcending religious, linguistic and regional or sectional diversities. Article 51 A

(f) further asks each citizen to value and preserve the rich heritage of our composite culture.

Especially, fraternity or brotherhood/ sisterhood is not alien to our multi-religious and multi-lingual culture. "Fraternity is indicative of a common bond or a feeling of unity between people or communities acting either with either private or public sphere."[53] The concept of liberty and equality would be more meaningful only in the context of fraternity. Promoting "dignity of the individual" and "unity and integrity of the nation" are the two objectives of fraternity. Orthodox church gave a place for a Hindu to be buried.

At Anari St. John's Orthodox Church, Muslims came to clean the mudded Church. By the time the work got over, it was time for 'Namaz', Muslim Prayer. And, the Church offered its space for the Muslims to do their Namaz. another incident where a Hindu Temple authorities offered their hall for Muslims to conduct Eid Namaz. Hindu was buried in Christian cemetery.

Public Spirituality

The use of Public theology is more than speaking and keeping the 'faith' in the public sphere. It focuses in particular on the ethical and political implications of religious self-understanding and life praxis. So, it is a critical thinking along with others concerning religious faith and public life.[54] *David Tacey in his book, The Spirituality Revolution: The Emergence of Contemporary Spirituality,* recognizes that we are in the midst of a genuine spiritual revival.[55] This public spirituality is not dogmatic in nature but addresses the common issues the people and nature face. I think that the future of religion depends on envisioning the genuine inter-religious spirituality. Today, inter-faith dialogue also sees the religious diversity not as a problem but as a promise, which positively contributes to mutual enrichment.

This contemporary phenomenon of public/secular spirituality seeks to integrate the natural and supernatural dimensions of human life meaningfully rather than searching for the proofs of God's existence or claiming monopoly over truth. In this context, the term "spirituality" does not discriminate between religion and denomination, or between believers and unbelievers. This brings us to post-secular holism.[56] Secular spirituality is therefore crucial because it goes beyond the religious spirituality and pre-fabricated notions. In Christianity, Jesus never subscribed to any religion but went beyond by questioning the religious dogmas and customs and focused on promoting fullness of life to all. He never separated people on the basics of religion. In secular spirituality there is openness, mutual trust and accommodation and it has a space for convergence of all religious faith communities, humanistic values and democratic principles.[57]

Critiques of secularism like Nandy and Madan also believe in the positive presence of religion in public. Inter-religious co-operation will help people to be religiously more tolerant towards other faiths and unite them in secular spirituality positively. This requires every religion to rediscover its public theology of religious harmony contextually. If the spirituality that religion poses is not making positive impacts in public in the context of injustice, exploitation and oppression it is not promoting genuine spirituality.

Perils of Fundamentalism and the Essentials of Fundamentals

Fundamentalism prevents the liberative praxis by powerful vested interests and it is not just a contention between religions but a ploy of socio-economic and political power. It prevents what religions can contribute to the secular concerns of liberation.[58] Bhargava views that, *"The Ram Janma Bhoomi Movement was less about God Ram and more about Hindu consolidation, less about building a temple and more about showing Muslims their place in a Hindu country."*[59] The Hindu nationalist makes use of *"memory, emotion, prejudice, religious differences"* etc... to advance their extremist agenda of external religious exclusion.[60] It is also taking religious fundamentalism as an instrument to keep the minority community under threat and fear. The need of the hour is therefore to liberate religion from the hands of the people who politicize it as an ideology. It demands the consensus within the secular forces and moderate thinkers of every religion who holds the fundamentals of religion.

As stated above, Nandy divides religion in to two aspects. One is religion-as-faith and the other, religion-as-ideology. For example, when political Hinduism or fundamentalist organizations of the *Sangh Parivar* speak about religion, they usually have in mind religion as an ideology. But the need of the hour is to project religion as faith, using the language of faith, love and religious tolerance. A discussion on faith and ideology in different religions will be rewarding if there is commitment and openness in them. Hence, there is a need to distinguish between what is religious fundamentalism and what are the fundamentals or the fundamental values of the religious scriptures. Selvanayagam has made a strong proposal in this regard.[61] He views that religious fundamentalism is one of the greatest threats in the world today. Fundamentalism breeds fanaticism and fanaticism breeds intolerance. "One of the fundamental characters of all forms of fundamentalism is lack of humility and openness, which militates against the sharing of faith in a spirit of dialogue."[62] But those who hold the fundamentals of the scriptures never allow their faith, love and hope to be overcome by fundamentalist trends.[63] In fundamentalism, there is a total ignorance of one's own scriptures and the scriptures of other faith traditions or religions.

The recovery of the fundamentals of faith in each religion would contribute to peace and harmony, which is the aim of inter-faith relation. Therefore, inter-religious dialogue is done not to intensify the ideological differences but to understand sympathetically other religious traditions and cooperate in issues that the society and people are struggling to cope with.

Christian Engagement with Secularism in India

God has made God's self-known and has convincingly acted in history for the renewal of humanity and society in Jesus of Nazareth. Jesus came to redeem humanity and established fulness of human dignity.[64] God's majesty and mystery can only be understood in historical events in the world. Through incarnation, God is in a manger, identified Godself with the common history as the prince of the worldly peace and a chief partner to human in common task. Abundance of life in the present is what has been promised by Him. P.D. Devanandan the first Director of Christian Institute for the Study of Religion and Society, Bangalore views that since new creation and new age is already the present reality and God is a God who works actively in history and is relational, it is right that Christians should involve in nation-building and actively participate in socio-political activities. He developed a theology of "New creation" which relates the unique revelation of God in the crucified and risen Christ to the universality of the historical movement of divine grace renewing persons, cultures and the cosmos. By quoting Ephesians 2: 14-16, he says, the cross of Jesus Christ breaks the hold of law (religion) and unites them in the new plane of being in Christ's new humanity. It also sends them back into their religions to critique and renew them in the light of their common humanity renewed in Christ. So, the cross of Jesus Christ is the vision of a common humanity transcending religions.[65] For Devanandan, the gospel is that, God who acted in Jesus renews the whole creation and that activity is continuing today in the spirit of the risen Jesus, re-creating humanity, and that at the end God will establish his kingdom on earth. The divine activity in Jesus for the world is from beginning to end a divine human activity, and therefore an integral part of secular history. Here the Church or the fellowship of the local congregation serves as the instrument of divine renewal.[66]

According to M.M. Thomas, realistic spirituality in a secular context could be evolved "by setting the politics of humanization of power-structures of society within the framework of a faith in and response to the New Humanity inaugurated by God in the Crucified and Risen Jesus Christ and being established in secular history through His spirit poured out on all mankind (sic)."[67] In seeking to narrate the meaning of Christ to the secular ideologies, he views that political theology can interpret prophetic spirituality that stands for liberation and humanization. Therefore, Christian theology has a mission to construct politics that should comprehend all religions based on non-violence and justice in order to humanize the world. The Church has the power to actualize the new humanity and - the true being of the Church is realized in its partnership with people of different faiths and no faith.[68] For Thomas, the secret of true humanism is to be found in the divine humanity of Christ and in his new creation. The mission of salvation and the task of humanization are integrally related to each other even if they cannot be considered identical.[69] He also urges the Christian community to exercise their prophetic core of Christian faith and contribute to the development of true humanism. He views that the process of secularization which is already at work in the world and the secular patterns of understanding human existence which has already emerged are themselves the product of the ferment of the Gospel working in traditional societies.[70] The constitutional democratic principles of liberty, equality, fraternity, justice and human dignity which shares the Gospel values would strengthen a harmonious society.

The Church should act as a partner in civil society and in secular *koinonia*. However, the Church is preoccupied with fundamentalism, dogmatic ideologies and conservatism which gives less chance for interrogation and participation in the secular space. Evolving a new non-communal,[71] borderless ecclesia of fellowship in Christ should be the focus of the Church in this context of cultural nationalism. Sathianathan Clarke, an Indian Christian theologian, views that in the context of competing fundamentalism, the Christian doctrine of

"Trinity… helps us mine a spaciousness within God that embraces all while lifting up the love of God as revealed in Jesus Christ."[72] Christians must discover fully what it means to be servants of Christ and stewards of God's mysteries, which apostle Paul describes in 1 Corinthians 4:1. The ecumenical affirmation of the belief that God is Trinity serves as the "grammar" or template for Christian reflection on God. It also affirms that God is communion rather than singular and it produces infinite space within God. This notion of God in three persons and the mysteries in this relationship of divine communion are dynamic, loving and overflowing. Hence, Christians are called to be stewards of this mystery of God.[73] In this context, Indian Christianity should be grounded in the reality of God in Trinity; Unity in Trinity and Trinity in Unity. In this context, Sahayadhas understand the Trinitarian communion of the Godhead as "a *network of mutually dependent relationships*, which transcends narrow particularism and embraces multiplicity and differences and its unique feature is the extension of its scope beyond the boundaries of the Church even to reach out to those who hatch hatred against the Church."[74]

Further, Archbishop Desmond Tutu views that confining God in to one religion or monopoly over God is in a real sense irreligious. He says, "To claim God exclusively for Christian is to make God too small and in a real sense blasphemous. God is bigger than Christianity and cares for more than Christians. He has to, if only for the simple reason that Christians are quite late arrivals on the world scene. God has been around since even before creation, and that is a very long time."[75] Countering this exclusivism, which was developed in the colonial missionary era and the triumphalist language of Christian theology and ecclesia in India must be revisited. For S. Kappen, ecclesiology is basically historical, that is Jesus of history. Therefore, he perceives Church as Jesus-fellowship and people's movements.[76] He noticed two forms of Church, they are dominant and emerging. Christian activists who are committed to the struggles of the poor for bread and freedom based on Jesus' message form the emerging Church of Jesus-fellowship, not the dominant ideology.[77] The Christians or the church should listen not only to the words contained in the Bible but also to the word operative in historical location, events and secular movements for individual rights and social peace etc.[78] Clarke opines that, "Counter-fundamentalist theology must offer a God who looks like the historical Jesus, one who generously embraces the well-being of the whole family."[79]

Selvanayagam believes that "one can be both evangelical and dialogical at the same time in the truest sense of the terms"[80] in a pluralistic context. Being evangelical does not mean being fundamentalist and being dialogical does not require to hold to fixed models about traditional divisions of exclusivism, inclusivism and pluralism,[81] but transcending all barriers. The universal love and fraternity embodied in the Christian scripture and the fraternity that is impeded in the preamble of the constitution could contribute reciprocally in for the harmonious living together when relationship in dialogue with religions is possible in everyday life. This calls for a secular pluralistic fraternity, in God's borderless love. That could be the future of our co-existence rather than subsumed by religio-cultural homogenization or ignoring secularism.

To envision a better society, inter-religious reformation with democratic principles, commitment to secular pluralistic fraternity, revisiting the collective self-confidence that prevailed in India, strengthening the secular spirituality that confronts religious fundamentalism and fundamentals of religion and perils of fundamentalism in the inter-religious relations are some of the ways forward.

Endnotes

[1] Charles Taylor, "Modes of Secularism," in *Secularism and its Critics,* edited by Rajeev Bhargava (Delhi: Oxford University Press, 1998), 31-32.

² The great cultural movement that began in Italy during the thirteenth century and spread all over the Europe is known as the Renaissance. Many of the concepts and ideas of the Middle ages were abandoned by the emergence of Renaissance. Medieval thinkers believed that the most important responsibility of the people was to pray to God to save their soul. Renaissance thinkers, on the contrary, believed that the people own a responsibility to the society in which they live. Thus, the study of theology which was an important subject in the middle ages was replaced by the study of humanity.

³ Sailen Debnath, *Secularism: Western and*, 38.

⁴ Himanshu Rai, *Secularism and its Colonial Legacy*, 24.

⁵ Rene Descartes was a French mathematician and scientist. He is generally considered father of Modern Western Philosophy.

⁶ Bryan R. Wilson, "Secularization, 159.

⁷ Frederique Apffel-Marglin, "Secularism, Unicity and diversity: The case of Haracandi's grove," in *Tradition Pluralism and Identity*, edited by Veena Das, Dipankar Gupta and Patricia Uberoi (New Delhi: Sage Publication, 1999), 75.

⁸ Satish Chandra, *Historiography, Religion and State*, 96-97.

⁹ Mukul Kesavan, *Secular Common Sense* (New Delhi: Penguin Books India Pvt Ltd, 2001), 4-5.

¹⁰ Asghar Ali Engineer, *Contemporary Politics of Identity, Religion and Secularism* (New Delhi: Ajanta Books International, 1999), 72-73.

¹¹ Amartya Sen, *The Argumentative Indian: Writings on Indian History, Culture and Identity* (London: Penguin Books, 2005), 16-17; Prateep K. Lahiri, *Decoding Intolerance*, 134.

¹² Asghar Ali Engineer, "Secularism in India-Theory and Practice," *Social Action* 44/1 (January-March, 1994): 1.

¹³ Amartya Sen, *The Argumentative Indian*, 19; Prateep K. Lahiri, *Decoding Intolerance*, 135.

¹⁴ Prateep K. Lahiri, *Decoding Intolerance*, 135.

¹⁵ Critics say that this saying was said to promote intra-religious harmony than inter-religious harmony; cited by Vincent Sekhar,S.J. *Building Strong Neighbourhoods*, 31.

¹⁶ Felix Wilfred, "On the Future of Asian Theologizing: A forward to Asian Public Theology," in *Theology Beyond Neutrality: Essays to Honour Wesley Ariyarajah*, edited by Marshal Fernando and Robert Crusz (Sri Lanka: The Ecumenical Institute for Study and Dialogue, 2011), 3-4.

[17] Felix Wilfred, "On the Future of Asian Theologizing, 5.

[18] Kiran Angra and Karamjeet Kaur, eds., *Relevance of Nehru's Thoughts* (New Delhi: Pragatisheel Prakashan, 2012), 181.

[19] Pannalal Dhar, *India and Her Democratic Problems: Religion, State and Secularism* (Calcutta: Punthi Pustak, 1993), 100.

[20]*The Constitution of India* -As modified up to the 1st August, 1975 (New Delhi: Government of India Ministry of Law, Justice and Company Affairs, 1975), 10; also see *The Constitution of India* -As modified up to 1st September, 1951, 13-14.

[21] Around 1870s, Arya Samaj was founded by Swami Dayananda Saraswati (1824-1883). The watch-word for Dayananda was "back to Vedas."

[22] Hindu Mahasaba was an organization representing various Hindu organizations formed in 1926.

[23] Hedgewar founded RSS in 1925. Its ideological development came with his successor M.S. Golwalkar.

[24] VHP was formed in 1964 by Swami Chinmayananda to consolidate and strengthen the Hindu society and its identity.

[25] Shiva Sana was formed in 1966 by Bal Thakeray in Mumbai. Gradually the party moved from solely advocating a Pro-Marathi ideology to support Hindu nationalistic agenda called Hindutva.

[26] M.S. Golwalkar, *Bunch of Thoughts* (Bangalore: Vikram Prakashan 4th Impression, 1968); M.S. Golwalkar, *We, or Our Nation Defined* (Nagpur: Bharat Publication 3rd Edition, 1945).

[27] Antony Kalliath, "Pilgrimage Identity of Christianity and the Emerging Religious Nationalism: An Analysis on the Political Trends in India," in *Pilgrims in Dialogue: A New Configuration of Religions for Millennium Community*, edited by Antony Kalliath (Bangalore: Dharmaram Publication, 2000), 229-230.

[28] "Delete Secular from the Constitution: Sena," http://www.thehansindia.com/posts/index/National/2015-01-29/Delete-secular-from-Constitution-Sena/128302 (15-10-2017).

[29] Partha S. Ghosh, *BJP and the Evolution of Hindu Nationalism: Savarkar to Vajpayee to Modi* (New Delhi: Manohar, 2nd edition 2017), 449-451.

[30] "Hindutva and Cow Terror: Politics of Hatred," Mainstream LVI/ 17 (April, 2018), http://www.mainstreamweekly.net/article7865.html (20-14-2018).

[31] T.K. Oommen, "Religious Nationalism and Democratic Polity in India," in *Nationalism and Hindutva: A Christian Response*, edited by Mark T.B. Laing (Delhi: ISPCK, 2005), 35, 45.

[32] T.N. Madan, *Modern Myths, Locked Minds*, 225.

[33] In the Indian Constitution, Laws relating to crime and punishment are uniform for all citizens. So are the laws relating to commerce, contracts and other economic affairs. However, family affairs such as marriage, divorce, inheritance, guardianship and adoption are legally permitted to be governed by customs or rules applicable to the persons and their religious community. This has been the practice from the time of the British rule, because it was considered prudent not to disturb the people's religious and community customs as far as their private affairs are concerned. The same position continued even after the independence and people were permitted to follow their respective personal laws. Today, Hindu Nationalists demand a Uniform Civil Code for all religions. Several liberal women's movements also argue that the Uniform Civil Code will give women more rights. This will be elaborated in the following chapters.

[34] "Cultural Nationalism Wins Over Pseudo-secularism," *Organiser* (December 24, 1995): 3; Shashi Tharoor, *Why I am A Hindu*, 188-189.

[35] "State Sponsored Communalism," Seminar 400 (December, 1992): 26.

[36] Rajan Gurukkal, "A Blindness About India," *Economic and Political Weekly* 49/49 (6 December, 2014):12-13.

[37]http://vidyabharti.net/EN/AimAndObjective (11-05-2017).

[38] Sanjay Asthana, "Religion and Secularism as Embedded Imaginaries: A Study of Indian Television Narratives," *Critical Studies in Media Communication* 25/3 (August, 2008): 305-307.

[39] Partha S. Ghosh, *BJP and the Evolution of Hindu Nationalism: From Periphery to Centre*, 212-213.

[40] Modern statecraft means scientific management of secular- institution. Rajeev Bhargava, ed., *Secularism and Its Critics* (Delhi: Oxford University Press, 1998), 22-23; Ashis Nandy, "The Politics of Secularism and the Recovery of Religious Tolerance," in *Secularism and its Critics,* edited by Rajeev Bhargava (Delhi: Oxford University Press, 1998), 324.

[41] T.N. Madan, "Secularism in its Place," in *Secularism and its Critics,* edited by Rajeev Bhargava (Delhi: Oxford University Press, 1998), 298.

[42] Neera Chandhoke, *Beyond Secularism*, 50.

[43] Neera Chandhoke, *Beyond Secularism, 50.*

⁴⁴ Neera Chandhoke, *Beyond Secularism*, 90.

⁴⁵ Neera Chandhoke, *Beyond Secularism*, 90.

⁴⁶ Neera Chandhoke, *Beyond Secularism*, 90-91, 301.

⁴⁷ Charles Taylor, "Modes of Secularism, 46.

⁴⁸ Hans Kung, *Global Responsibility: In Search of a New World Ethic* (Munich: SCM Press, 1990), 76.

⁴⁹ Felix Wilfred, "Inter-Religious Dialogue as a Political Quest," in *Pilgrims in Dialogue: A New Configuration of Religions for Millennium Community*, edited by Antony Kalliath (Bangalore: Dharmaram Publication, 2000), 31-50.

⁵⁰ T.K. Oommen, *State and Society in India,* 123.

⁵¹ http://indianexpress.com/article/india/india-news-india/bhartiya-muslim-mahila-andolan-ups-first-woman-qazi-demands-immediate-ban-on-practice-of-triple-talaq-2829049/ (June 11, 2016).

⁵² http://edition.cnn.com/2017/05/18/asia/triple-talaq-supreme-court/index.html (10-10-2017).

⁵³cited by Smaran Shetty and Tanaya Sanyal, "Fraternity and the Constitution: A Promising Beginning in the Nandini Sundar vs State of Chattisgarh,"(NUJS Law Review, July- September 2011), http://nujslawreview.org/wp-content/uploads/2016/12/smaran-shetty-and-tanaya-sanyal.pdf (10-02-2018).

⁵⁴David Bromell, "What is public theology?," (University of Otago: Centre for Theology and Public Issues, May 2011) http://www.otago.ac.nz/ctpi/otago032508.pdf (25-04-2016).

⁵⁵ David Tacey, *The Spirituality Revolution: The Emergence of contemporary Spirituality* (New York: Routledge, 2004), 1-2.

⁵⁶Cornel W du Toit, "Secular spirituality versus secular dualism: Towards post secular holism as model for a natural theology," http://hts.org.za/index.php/HTS/article/viewFile/416/316 (30-04-2016).

⁵⁷Indukuri John Mohan Razu, *Secular Spirituality: Contesting the Aberrations of Religiosity* (Bangalore: Candid Publication, 2014), 76-77.

⁵⁸Bipan Chandra, *Communalism in Modern India* (Delhi: Vikas, 1987), cited by S. Arokiasamy, S.J. "Theology of Religions from Liberative Perspectives," in *Religious Pluralism: An Indian Christian Perspective,* edited by Kuncheria Pathil (Delhi: ISPCK, 1999), 312.

⁵⁹ Rajeev Bhargava, *The Promise of India's Secular,* 229.

⁶⁰ Mukul Kesavan, *Secular Common Sense,* 94, cited by Rajeev Bhargava, *The Promise of India's Secular,* 230.

[61] see Israel Selvanayagam, *Being Evangelical and Dialogical*, 187-194.

[62] Israel Selvanayagam, *Being Evangelical and Dialogical*, 193-194.

[63] Israel Selvanayagam, *Being Evangelical and Dialogical*, 194.

[64] M.M. Thomas and T.K. Thomas, eds., *The Secular Witness of E.V. Mathew* (Madras: CLS, 1972), xiv.

[65] P.D. Devanandan, *Preparation for Dialogue: A Collection of Essays on Hinduism and Christianity in New India*, edited by Nalini Devanandan and M.M. Thomas (Bangalore: CISRS, 1964), 114.

[66] M.M. Thomas, *Risking Christ for Christ's Sake: Towards an Ecumenical Theology of Pluralism* (Geneva: WCC Publications, 1987), 87-88.

[67] M.M. Thomas, *The Secular Ideologies of India and the Secular Meaning of Christ* (Madras: CLS, 1976), 84.

[68] P.G. George and Y.T. Vinayaraj, eds., *Reclaiming Manyness: Re-reading M.M. Thomas in the Light of Indian Christian Theologies* (Serampore: SATHRI, 2015), 195-196.

[69] M.M. Thomas, *Salvation and Humanisation: Some Crucial Issues of the Theology of Mission in Contemporary India* (Madras: CLS, 1971), 8.

[70] M.M. Thomas, *Salvation and Humanisation*, 12.

[71] P.G. George and Y.T. Vinayaraj, eds., *Reclaiming Manyness*, 192.

[72] Sathianathan Clarke, *Competing Fundamentalism: Violent Extremism in Christianity, Islam, and Hinduism* (Louisville: Westminster John Knox Press, 2017), 178.

[73] Sathianathan Clarke, *Competing Fundamentalism*, 178-179.

[74] R. Sahayadhas, *Hindu Nationalism and the Indian Church: Towards an Ecclesiology in Conversation with Martin Luther* (New Delhi: Christian Imprints, 2016), 324-325.

[75] Desmond Tutu, *God Is Not Christian: And Other Provocations* (New York: HarperOne, 2011), 14.

[76] S. Kappen, "The Jesus Fellowship," *Jeevadhara* vol. 23 (September-October, 1974): 190.

[77] cited by Sam Varghese, "New Insights of Ecclesiology in Sabastian Kappen's Understanding," *Master's College Theological Journal* 1/1 (March, 2011): 62.

[78] S. Kappen, "Church and the Challenges of Social Revolution of Kerala," *Vaidikamithram* 3/1 (1969): 42, cited by Sam Varghese, "New Insights of Ecclesiology in Sabastian Kappen's Understanding, 62.

[79] Sathianathan Clarke, *Competing Fundamentalism*,178.

[80] Israel Selvanayagam, *A Second Call: Ministry and Mission in a Multifaith Milieu*, 189.

[81] Israel Selvanayagam, *A Second Call: Ministry and Mission in a Multifaith Milieu*, 9.

15

Building a Spiritually Mature and an Emotionally Strong Church

Samson Gandhi

This paper is a summary of the research findings reported in my doctoral thesis on the state of Christian counselling ministry in the Church in India. The purpose of my research is to call attention of the Church in India to the causes for concern in the area of spiritual, emotional and psychological well-being of the church and sensitize it to the opportunities for growth.

Who will benefit from this pamphlet?

The heads of the churches, both denominational and non-denominational, that make the policy decisions at the highest levels will benefit from this work. Specifically,

- Pastors and lay leaders will find guidelines in designing counselling training programs in their churches.

- Bible colleges will find it helpful in modifying their existing courses or designing new courses that are tailor-made to suit the current needs.

- Counselling agencies that offer counselling services and counselling training programs will also benefit in mobilizing their resources to assist the churches.

- Mission organizations that plant churches will benefit from its findings in making sure that counselling is part of the church fabric right from the beginning.

Statement of the Problem

India with an ever-increasing population of 1324 million has emerged a major player on the world stage. Its influence increases in various spheres like armed forces, diplomatic ties, IT skills, literacy and exports. India is one of the fastest growing economies and it is becoming increasingly urban. Such rapid growth is not without its fall-out. The middle-class population of India is most affected psychologically, emotionally and spiritually. The society at large and the Church is unable to deal with emotional fallout in the families thereby affecting the social fabric of the country. Life in cities is *"characterized by transience (short-time relations), superficiality (impersonal and formal relations with limited number of people), anonymity (not knowing the names and lacking intimacy), and individualism (people giving more importance to one's own personal interests)."*[1] Such breakdown of relationships and lack a community feeling has led many in cities into an alienated living.

The family structure has also changed radically. Nuclear families today have no support of extended families. Parents are engrossed in individual careers leaving little energy to invest in their relationship and child care. Psychologically, stress levels have increased. As a result, diseases such as diabetes, hyper tension and allergies have become common. Emotionally, people have become disconnected, insecure and unstable. The increasing number of suicides and divorces are alarming.

In 2010, the minister of law and justice declared there were 55,000 divorce cases pending in the country's courts.[2] World Health Organization (WHO) classifies India as the 'depression capital of the world.'[3] The problem is compounded with a shocking deficit of psychiatrists to the tune of seventy-seven per cent.[4] The government has taken several measures to address mental health issues arising from academic pressures and divorces. These measures include building mass awareness, removing social stigma attached to mental health issues, having counsellors at educational institutions and in police stations to deal with abuse in the families. Mediation teams are attached to the family courts to counsel with the disputing couples and prevent divorces.

While Christians face the same challenges as the world, the church at large lacks that ability to connect the gospel to ground realities. To keep faith amid raging spiritual battles in the marketplace, one needs more than a Sunday sermon. There are many ways the church provides spiritual nurture. However, not much is done to address personal issues at one-to-one level. Leaders of existing ministries have little time due to their other pressing responsibilities or have not been trained to deal with individuals battling problems that affect spiritual and emotional health. Several churches offer some form of counselling. But rarely does a church or a ministry put a program of counselling in place for the benefit of the members.

Does the church need a counselling ministry?

A tremendous initiative is currently underway to evangelize and plant churches across the country. However, although the numbers of churches are increasing, spiritual maturity of the members is a cause for concern; one of the main reasons being that emotional and psychological needs are not addressed adequately. As a result of evangelism, someone said, people walk through the front door of the church, but walk out of the back door due to lack of adequate pastoral care and counselling in the church. The Christian leadership in India is faced with the reality of rising incidence of abuse, divorce, suicides and depression within the church. Adverse effects of services offered outside of a biblical frame work cannot be ignored. Alternative therapies like Reiki healing, Transcendental Meditation, Feng shui, etc., offer short term relief for some and draw the members away from the church. There are dangers within the churches when members are offered quick-fix solutions that are not biblically sound. The Church must make every effort to minister to the members and keep them from seeking solutions outside the biblical frame work.

My research indicates that within the church of India, there is an:

- Ardent desire for personal counselling that is Biblical yet offered in a professional manner. Sixty-five per cent of the respondents indicated they would seek the services of trained counsellors in the church, if such services are provided.

- Adequate services to minister to personal needs of the members is lacking within the Church. While all churches I interviewed, believe the church has a role in building and maintaining the emotional health of the members, a mere fourteen per cent were comfortable with the services offered by the church.

- Absence of trained counsellors in the church. Less than half of the churches have a policy for counseling and only one third have training for counsellors in the churches.

Biblical Mandate for Counseling Ministry

Jesus showed how to do ministry and invited his disciples to pray to the Lord of the harvest that he may send out laborers (Matthew 9:35-38). As Ray Bakke puts it, Jesus' model of ministry involved visiting . . . so we go to people, teaching . . . so we plant schools, preaching . . . so we plant churches and healing all diseases of the people . . . so we plant clinics and hospitals. So, church planting alone cannot fulfil the expectations of the shared practice of Jesus. I would say even counseling centres can be places of healing.

Biblical Basis for Counseling

The Old Testament is replete with examples of counseling. In the New Testament, Jesus leads His own as the Good Shepherd. He also appointed under shepherds to care for other sheep. This has a distinct context within the Church where we are called to encourage one another, exhort one another, and confess to one another and be healed. Jesus promised and sent another *Paraclete*, the Holy Spirit who would continue His presence and ministry. The Holy Spirit is the real Counsellor.

The Holy Spirit gifts and empowers us for work in this ministry. As Christian Counsellors, we are co-workers with the wonderful Counsellor- the Holy Spirit. He gives continuity between Christ's ministry and that of His followers. Christian counseling is the ministry of Christians, seeking to come alongside another person to help cope with the problems of life, in accordance with the Word of God and the guidance of the Holy Spirit. God expects all of us, as Christians, to come alongside and help people spiritually. Some of us have the gifting and the call to develop the counseling ministry.

Biblical Clarity on Suffering

Pain is a common denominator for all suffering. It serves well as a warning bell whether it is physical or psychological. But many times, pain is misunderstood for suffering. Instead of addressing the larger issue of suffering, pain is treated evidently with poor results.

God gives us an understanding of suffering and how to address it through the life of Job. Job's three friends come together to counsel with Job. They seem to have brought the best of 'psychology' with them. Having heard of Job's suffering they left their zone of comfort and travelled to see him. It may seem that making appointments is a modern-day practice but Eliphaz, Bildad and Zophar were business-like and even professional for they "met together by an appointment". They were clear in their goals "to sympathize and comfort him". They were genuine and authentic in identifying with Job. They wept aloud, tore their robes and sprinkled dust on their heads. Best of all they sat on the ground *with* him for seven days and seven nights (Job 2:11-13). From a counseling psychology point of view, they seem to have done the best. But the three friends of Job were found to be acutely deficient in the sight of God. Twice in these three verses, God says, "You have not spoken of me what is right, as my servant Job has." It is evident from this that, "Right theology comes before right psychology (Job 42:7-9)."

At a time when the church is faced with innumerable therapies and alternative therapies some even from the new age stock, it is important to have right theology. Many lose their faith when they can't make meaning of suffering. The greatest risk is when people perceive their suffering as undeserved. A lay person is even more susceptible to wrong theology when they are bombarded with wrong theologies behind prosperity gospel, 'name it and claim it' and word faith movement. Every counsellor must exercise due diligence in developing a sound, balanced and biblical theology or else be judged by their own counselees.

Like with suffering, counsellors must also develop biblically sound theology for every aspect of people's problems. Pre-marital relationships, marriage, divorce and remarriage, parenting, abortion, finances, role and responsibilities in the church, work and ministry are a few other aspects where we need to have a biblical rationale. For lack of proper teaching on these and other aspects people are going astray. Like it is said in Jeremiah, "My people are destroyed for lack of knowledge. Christian counsellors should be able to bring that knowledge of God to the counseling room.

Jesus is our example and model. "His ministry of healing and reconciliation brought God "out of the temple" and put Him on the streets. It was the ministry of Jesus that united the divine heart with the human hand that shed tears of compassion."[5]

Can counseling lead to transformation?

On the road to Emmaus, Jesus offers a blueprint of counseling as He joined the confused and dejected disciples, Cleopas and his co-traveller. He came alongside, walked with them, and showed His willingness to meet them at the point of their need. Beginning with exploration of their situation, engaging their emotions and challenging their misbeliefs with His robust theology, He began the process of stimulating the change in their thinking and behaviour. He explained, taught and got close to them emotionally and spiritually. So much so that their hearts were burning as He taught them. He left them free to respond. But what Jesus did spur them on to action and moved them to a point of independence. Luke 24: 13-27. People may or may not see a vision of Christ; they surely would like to see a bit of Jesus in every counsellor.

If how He conversed with Cleopas and his friend showed us the process of counseling, what He said while counseling with Nicodemus, the woman He met at Sychar in Samaria, Zacchaeus, the tax collector, the woman caught in adultery and the rich young ruler, will provide a pattern to counsel for the transformation of the church. Can a one-off counseling session like Jesus had with them bring about lasting transformation of those individuals and lead to transformation of the church?

Spiritual Transformation- John 3:1ff

Nicodemus was a spiritual leader of his time. He was a Pharisee and a member of the Sanhedrin, the Jewish ruling council. Yet, he was searching and seeking. Probably for political reasons, he sought Jesus in the privacy of the night. Jesus received him and offered confidentiality. Unlike today's leaders, he had no compulsion to make it a matter for public 'testimony for the glory of God.' Nicodemus was attracted to Jesus. He said: "Rabbi, we know you are a teacher who has come from God. For no one could perform the miraculous signs you are doing if God were not with him." Leaders come for counselling to those whom they perceive as having God being with them.

Yet Jesus side-stepped the personal praise offered to Him and addressed what Nicodemus needed to address. He puts it as it is when He says: "Most assuredly, I say to you, unless one is born again, he cannot see the kingdom of God." John 3:3. Then He goes on to explain how one can be born again. We do not see an immediate transformation, but it was evident when Nicodemus stood and 'defended' Jesus in the Sanhedrin for being condemned without a fair trial. He later goes with Joseph of Arimathea to Pilate to ask for the body of Jesus. Contrast his bold venture with how the disciples abandoned Jesus. One 'counselling session' changed Nicodemus so much that it impacted the entire community of his day and even us as we try to understand what it means to be born again. Jesus used counselling to shape the spiritual leaders of His time. Apostles have done it; can we do any less. It is possible today and very much needed too.

Social Transformation

The woman of Samaria stands in stark contrast to Nicodemus. Read John 4:4ff. She is a woman with hardly any rights; she belongs to a rebel group living a self-protective life away from stone-throwing community. Five times married but living in a live-in relationship therefore spurned by society. Jesus crossed social and cultural boundaries to break man-made walls of prejudice, discrimination and exploitation. He broke religious, gender and social barriers at an impromptu 'counseling session' with her by the well. Jesus knew her thirst for the Messiah and hurts inflicted upon her from a cruel community. He took time to build up a relationship, debating with her and offering the hope of better things. After getting her attentive ear, He took time to offer her a fulfilling life. She was so completely overwhelmed by His love that she runs back to the villagers she was avoiding and invites them to go and see the man who told her everything she ever did and did not condemn.

One counseling session with one woman seems to have transformed an entire village. India needs this model not just for rural villages but also for urban concrete villages. Christian counseling can bring about a social transformation.

Economic Transformation – Luke 19:1-9

Zacchaeus the tax collector faced hostility all his working life and was desperate for acceptance. He did an unthinkable thing for a man of his stature; he climbed a sycamore tree to get a glimpse of Jesus. He was rejected and isolated by his own people but invited by Jesus Himself for a meal. In Jewish culture, sharing a meal is an ultimate expression of acceptance.

Counseling is offering acceptance. Jesus' acceptance liberates Zacchaeus from his bondages for he spontaneously announced, "Look, Lord, I give half of my goods to the poor; and if I have taken anything from anyone by false accusation, I restore fourfold." As a result, a redistribution of wealth was taking place. Jesus declared salvation to him and his household. And salvation was being experienced by the poor in another form for their basic needs were being met by the sharing in the kingdom of God. Once again, we see powerful outcome of a counseling session. This time it brought about economic transformation.

Redemptive Justice – John 8:3ff

Jesus' attitude and action towards the woman who was caught in adultery presents the four facets of His ministry. We can see that Jesus acts like a 'King' and therefore protects her. He contends for her and shields her from self-righteous, bigoted religious fanatics. Secondly, Jesus took up her legal case as it were and argues for her and wins the case. He turns the table on her accusers, and they leave her alone. Thirdly, Jesus plays the role of a priest whose job was to secure forgiveness for the sins of the people he ministers.   He is so kind, that he does not even make her feel that He was doing her a great service in forgiving her sins. Lastly, with no hint of condemnation Jesus as a 'Wonderful Counsellor' exhorts her to go and 'sin no more.' He rendered justice but to redeem. Through the forgiven woman, He gave hope to all the exploited and those struggling with challenges of righteous living.

Jesus counselled with people and they were transformed, and they went on to impact others. The Pastors and the trained counsellors can do the same, today.

For this change and growth to occur, the Church can draw from the work of many counsellors in this field.

Eminent counsellors like Dr. Larry Crabb, Rev Selwyn Hughes, Siang-Yang Tan, Mike Sheldon and Dave Ames, Isaac and Shirley Lim, and Dr. Gary Collins have worked extensively in understanding the counseling needs of the church and the church's response. Although they address issues in Asia and across the Atlantic, we can draw a few lessons from their long and hard work in the ministry of Christian counseling.

Insights gained from literature review

- Pulpit ministry is not adequate to meet personal needs of people in the church. The church must have an intentional strategy in bringing relief and resolution to personal problems. If church is a community of caring members, then it is the best place for people to find comfort and counsel for their personal problems where committed and caring members are equipped to counsel with other members.[6]

- Personal problems arise when the innermost needs of being loved, accepted, meaning and purpose to life are not realized. The spiritual gifts given by the Holy Spirit to each member are to be exercised in serving others for people to experience the fruit of the Spirit - love, joy, peace, patience, kindness, goodness, faithfulness, gentleness and self-control. The church is in a strong position to play a defining role in the spiritual and emotional well-being of the people.

- Pastoral ministry involves counseling. The pastor, regardless of training, does not enjoy the privilege of electing whether to will counsel or not. Inevitably, people bring their problems to the pastor for the best guidance and wisest care. This is an important part of pastoral ministry. The choice is not between counseling and not counseling, but between counseling in a disciplined and skilled way and counseling in an undisciplined and unskilled way.[7] Training is essential for pastors and lay members to be skilled counsellors. The church must resume its responsibility in equipping members in biblical counseling and change the church into counseling and caring community. Training committed Christians in the church to handle a good deal of the counseling load could see an increase in spiritual and emotional maturity in our churches.[8]

- Proficiency of Lay counsellors cannot be undermined as they achieve clinical outcomes equal to or significantly better than those obtained by professionals. Hence lay counseling must be an important part of the church's work and ministry.[9]

- Perimeter of Christian counseling does not pertain only to Christians. Counseling with non-believers is a good way of building a rapport. A Christian counsellor must approach counseling with non-Christians sensitively and cautiously. Done with discretion, and leading by example, counseling can lead to sharing of the gospel.

- Psychology can be integrated with theology by combing insights from psychology and psychotherapy so long as it passes the judgment bar of Scripture. Larry Crabb terms this approach as 'spoiling the Egyptians'[10]

- Program to train lay counsellors needs to be designed with due emphasis on proper selection, supervision, maintaining boundaries, making suitable referrals when faced with complicated problems and evaluation of lay Christian counsellors. Of the various models of counseling, churches can consider a suitable model that best fits their needs.

The Role of the Church

Four questions people generally ask when faced with personal problems, namely:

1. What's wrong?

2. Who can help?

3. What will the helper do?

4. What can I hope for if I do seek help?[11]

While the above questions can be asked by anyone, they assume a unique significance when asked by Christians in the unique setting of a church. Is the church equipped to answer these questions?

What's wrong?

Many spiritually minded people over-generalize and attribute all personal problems to sin. This is but one cause for personal problems. Selwyn Hughes classifies various approaches to understanding human problems:

i.   Moral Model: People have made wrong choices and need to be challenged and confronted. For example: Jesus counselling with Martha.

ii. Recovery model: People have been humiliated and need to be affirmed. Like Jesus counsels with Zacchaeus, the Tax Collector.

iii. Spiritual model: People have been overcome by the effects of indwelling sin and need the therapy of prayer and spiritual surrender. For example: Jesus was counselling with woman caught in adultery.

iv. Deliverance model: People have been afflicted by evil spirits and need to be delivered. This is clear in the case of the demon possessed man in Gadarenes.

v.   Medical model: People have been damaged by others and life and need expert psychological repairs.[12] God working with Elijah is an example of this.

"Who can help?"

The five approaches show us that caregivers need insights at different levels and at varying depths. There was a time when the Pastor was the most educated man and was trusted implicitly. However, over the last few decades, pastors have been overwhelmed with regular church services and administrative work or lacked training and therefore not competent to address the personal problems. Today more people who are trained in theology and psychology bring the best of both to the well-being of the church. Members of a caring community can counsel at three different levels.[13] All of us are called to encourage one another and some would be trained to exhort, and a few others are called to enlighten helping people with deep rooted problems.

"What will the helper do?"

Although people have genuine expectations, they also have apprehensions and sometimes misgivings about the counselling process. Naaman did not consider Elisha a professional because his treatment was simple and not even personal. Moreover, the consultation was free. Likewise, Christian counselling that is offered under the banner of the church and free of cost may be looked down upon but can be effective.

Christian counselling offers holiness but not necessarily happiness. As someone said, "In life there are no easy solutions, but only difficult choices." A counsellor is required to exercise caution and discernment and not fall into traps of mediation, abuse of a spiritual position, or giving advice without exploration of the problem. Counsellors need to be flexible and use an appropriate approach depending on the culture and personality of the individual. There cannot be one size fits all approach and usually counselling is eclectic in nature.

"What can I hope for if I do seek help?"

1. People change if they are willing to wrestle with God and with other human beings about the deep matters of the heart.

2. People change to the degree they are drawn into an intimate relationship with God and other human beings.

3. People change to the degree they obediently walk in the path of the royal law of love based on the wonder of being forgiven.[14]

In other words when people seek a change as a result of counselling, they should be prepared to be 'disturbed', 'connected' and 'directed'.

In conclusion, people need to be disturbed from their obsessive, adamant pursuit of life outside of Christ, connected by a non-judgemental, accepting and loving relationship with the counsellor in order to be directed to taste the Lord and live a life that is pleasing to the Lord. Much of counseling that was offered in the early church was pastoral care and pastoral counseling. Pastoral counseling is taught in all under-graduate theological degree courses. Several colleges offer Master of Theology with a counseling concentration, but we seldom see it practiced in a systematic way in the Church. The increase in problems related to marriage, family, academics, parenting, depression, behaviour, spiritual guidance, self-care, grief and addictions echo the cry for better counseling in the Church. David L. Smith puts it aptly:

Because the family is the essential building block of society, and because of an ever-increasing attack on the institution of marriage and family, an important part of the discipling process must be a strong emphasis on healthy marriages and families. Counseling young people on relationships with the opposite sex should begin early in adolescence, long before marriage.[15]

The Church must reclaim its ministry to the soul. Christ the head of the Church seeks to minister and offer abundant life.

Research Findings

A survey conducted among Bishops, Pastors and Leaders of churches from various denominations to understand the counseling services offered in churches in Hyderabad, the approach taken in providing these services and the nature of training programs to train pastors and lay leaders revealed the following:

- All church leaders believe that the church has a role in building and maintaining the emotional health of the members of the church through counseling, however they were not comfortable with what is offered or how it is offered to the members

- Significant part of counseling is done by pastors. Only ten per cent professional counseling is currently being done.

- Less than half the churches interviewed had a policy for counseling

- Although only seventy-one per cent of church leaders received any training for counseling as part of their theological training all expressed a desire for additional training

- The biggest issues facing churches are administrative, spiritual and emotional

- Seventy-nine per cent of the church leaders desire the assistance of a trained team of counsellors

- More than seventy per cent of the churches do not have regular training courses in counseling

- Sixty-four per cent of churches wanted training programs for counseling

The above findings reflect the growing awareness that there is a problem and the disparity between offering a counseling training program in churches and Christian institutions that will be able to solve the problem. There is an urgent need for theological colleges and churches to start designing courses to prepare graduates and church leaders to address the counseling needs of the Church, which has begun to face serious marketplace stresses and strains. Providing biblical counseling in a biblical frame work with a strong support from the church community will significantly increase the emotional well-being of the members of the church.

The leaders of the church and the members are witnessing increasing numbers, of divorces, suicides, cases of depression, sexual abuse and physical abuse within the church.

Although depression is known as a silent killer, globally, India is just waking to the reality that many people even do not know that they are suffering with depression. Although India has one of the lowest divorce rates it is facing a severe attack on its families. The findings of a survey show that

- People seek help and they do so from friends when faced with a personal problem. Fifty-five per cent people would turn to a friend in church while twenty seven percent from one outside church. Only four per cent were indifferent

- When faced with specific problems more than fifty per cent would seek the help of a friend in the church. The other fifty per cent would seek the help of a trained Christian counsellor or a pastor

Table 1: Choice of Helper for various problems

Sl. No.	Helper	Marital	Parenting	Emotional problem	Personal problem
1	Personal/ Family friend	52	51	64	61
2	A psychologist who is a counsellor	2	6	2	3
3	My pastor	23	22	14	26
4	A trained Christian counsellor	27	29	28	17
5	Any other	11	10	10	11
6	No answer	8	11		

Figure 1

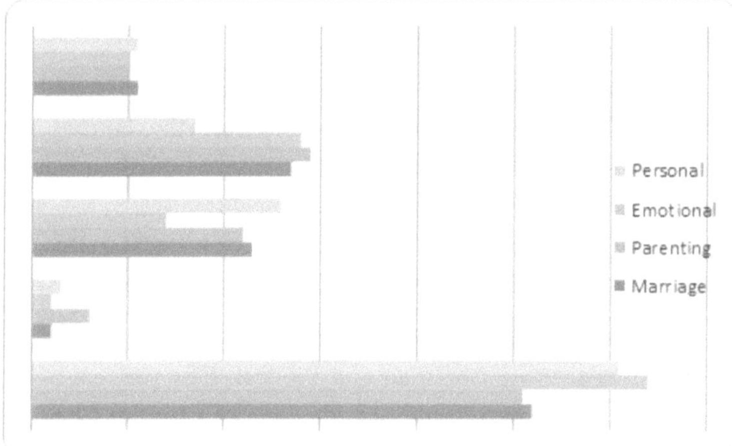

- Nearly sixty per cent of church members are comfortable seeking help from friends. If such friends can be trained in the basics of counseling, the church will benefit a lot

- Pastors and Trained Christian counsellors are the next preferred counsellors. They are approached when the problems are more specific and perhaps more complicated. This is another great window of opportunity to strengthen the Church

- The church members are still not comfortable to seek the help of a professional psychologist. Pastors and trained counsellors can make a big difference in this attitude if they are trained in making proper referrals

- Another finding was that while ninety-two per cent of the respondents were 'satisfied' with their experience of receiving help in the past, an overwhelming ninety three percent of the members desire to have trained counsellors in the church

Suggestions

11 Steps to a Spiritually Mature and Emotionally Strong Church

The survey among church leaders and church members has established that there is a real need for training in counseling in the churches. The church leaders would like to have trained counselors and the members would like to seek the services of such trained counselors. Based on the survey the following is proposed to create a viable counseling ministry model to meet this crucial need of counseling in the church.

1. **Acknowledge the need for the church to provide counseling services** that are Christian and Biblical. Fifty per cent of the members surveyed would seek the help of a trained Christian counselor or a pastor. Ninety three percent expressed their desire to have trained counselors in the church. There is an obvious need for professional counselling in current times when individuals and families are under tremendous spiritual, emotional and psychological stresses leading to unprecedanted numbers of divorce, suicides and lifestyle diseases.

2. **Bring out a clear policy to provide an effective ministry of counseling.** This will help the people involved in the important ministry of counseling to follow some standard procedures / principles and maintain a healthy standard of confidentiality, trust and avoid unnecessary problems and complications.

3. **Continuing Professional Development for Pastors is essential** to make them transformational leaders. Pastors have expressed an overwhelming desire to receive specialized counseling training to add to the pastoral counseling training received in their theological colleges. A foundational course designed with biblical principles on family counseling, and specialized modules on marriage, pre-marital and parenting counseling among others would enable the pastors to provide effective counseling.

4. **Develop a counseling team**. Pastors who have large congregations have expressed their need for the assistance of trained counsellors. Mature members in different age groups could be trained to become counsellors at three different levels.

    a. **Encouragement** – person has basic training in counseling, and is therefore able to relate well, listen attentively and provide immediate comfort and encouragement. They are also able to pray sensitively into the problem situation. Such training must be provided to care cell leaders, youth advisors and small group leaders.

    b. **Exhortation** – the counsellor is trained to build someone up using the reliable and trustworthy principles in God's word. It involves the ability to wisely apply scripture to day to day life situations and help counselees in their problem situations.

    c. **Enlightenment** - these counsellors have the necessary spiritual and psychological training to bring about enlightenment in the minds of the counselees that can free them from problem situations. They assist the understanding of underlying causes of problems and exposing false belief systems in the light of the scriptural principles.

5. **Educate the church on the benefits of biblical counseling**, dangers of counseling based on secular values and questionable new age therapies. This will build an interest among members to seek counseling from pastors and trained Christian counsellors. The church could observe one Sunday every year as a Counseling Sunday to build awareness. Counseling issues can be highlighted in newsletters, magazines and sermons.

6. **Formulate counseling training programs in Churches** that are appealing, enjoyable, and effective. Matters of doctrine, balance in courses content, competency of facilitators and training methodology are important in designing a counsellor training

course. Since time is a constraint courses can have a balance of self-study and facilitated learning during face to face contact. Pastors and senior counsellors can be trained in specialized modules on pre-marital counseling, marriage counseling, parenting, and grief counseling. Courses dealing with depression, suicidal tendencies and behavioural problems can be offered to experienced senior counsellors who are willing to receive sustained training.

7. **Good training is valuable and expensive**. However, such expenditure is an investment in the spiritual well-being of the church members. Choose members who have a commitment to Christ, loyal to the local church, have a heart to counsel people, can maintain confidentiality and are willing to offer their services to the church to be trained as counsellors.

8. **Harness counseling ministry as a blessing to the community**. Churches in India are experiencing increasing resistance to evangelism. Counseling is an effective way of meeting people at the level of their felt need. This opens doors to present the goodness of the gospel and be open to the work of the Spirit in leading them to Christ.

9. **Include seminaries /Bible colleges and counseling agencies along with churches**, to come together and provide the best of counseling training to the pastors and church counsellors to make the Church in India spiritually mature and emotionally strong. A specialized course can be introduced, and a department established in all theological institutions in India to train Christian counsellors, exclusively.

10. **Just remember that care is required for caregivers as well**. Pastors bogged down by administrative concerns and pastoral care are likely to face burnout. A systematic approach to counseling within the churches should include adequate safeguards both for the counselors and the members who seek counseling. Supervision of

counsellors ensures counsellors' accountability and effectiveness apart from offering such safe spaces to process issues in their own life and ministry. Pastors need the services of counsellors also.

11. **Key to successful counseling ministry is guided by accreditation** by a professional body. Association of Christian Counsellors (South Asia) has been formed in the year 2000 to provide accreditation services to Christian counsellors, counseling agencies that provide training courses and counseling services and represent the body of Christian counsellors to the government. Pastors and lay leaders involved in counseling can move a level higher in their transformational leadership through accreditation. This is one of the best practices that churches can consider building into its system.

I pray that the leaders of the Church, both men and women in India will bring about such a transformation and, in the process, become transformational leaders.

Endnotes

[1] Kumar, *Urban Sociology* (Agra: Lakshimi Narain Agarwal, 2001. Christ & Cities Transformation of urban centers, (Chennai: Mission Educational Books, 2005), 75.

[2] *DNA – Daily News and Analysis* 24 June 2010

[3] http://articles.timesofindia.indiatimes.com/2011-07-27/india/29820227_1_depression-lifetime-income

[4] http://www.globalissues.org/news/2011/09/10/11124

[5] Advanced Biblical Counselling, a Level 1 course offered by 'Person to Person', India, 8

[6] Lawrence J. Crabb, *Effective Biblical Counselling: Model for Helping Caring Christians Become Capable Counsellors* (Grand Rapids: Zondervan Publishing House, 1977), 15.

[7] Gary Collins, *Christian Counselling: A Comprehensive Guide Rev. Ed.* (Dallas: Word Publishing, 1988), 16.

8 Lawrence J. Crabb, *Effective Biblical Counselling: Model for Helping Caring Christians Become Capable Counsellors* (Grand Rapids: Zondervan Publishing House, 1977), 15.

9 Selwyn Hughes, *A Friend In Need: How to Help People Through Their Problems* (England: Kingsway Publications Ltd., 1981), 14.

10 Lawrence J. Crabb, *Effective Biblical Counselling: Model for Helping Caring Christians Become Capable Counsellors* (Grand Rapids: Zondervan Publishing House, 1977), 47.

11 Lawrence J. Crabb & Dan B. Allender, *Hope When You Are Hurting,* (Michigan: Zondervan Publishing House, 1996), 17.

12 Crusade for World Revival, *An Introduction to Christian Counseling,* (Course Manual, Surrey 2000), 5.

13 Lawrence J. Crabb, *Effective Biblical Counselling: Model for Helping Caring Christians Become Capable Counsellors* (Grand Rapids: Zondervan Publishing House, 1977), 97.

14 Lawrence J. Crabb & Dan B. Allender, *Hope When You Are Hurting,* (Michigan: Zondervan Publishing House, 1996), 155.

15 David L. Smith, *All God's People: a theology of the church,* (Illinois: Victor Books, 1996), 415.

16

Towards a Borderless Medical Mission

Sheeja Noone

The aim of medical mission has always been to give aid in the form of building hospitals and to give medical aid to heal the body. It is also involved in training people to be health givers and caregivers. Medical mission has also ventured into preventive medicine, health education and research. The organised body came into being in India in 1902, and was called the Medical missionaries of India. It was renamed as Christian Medical Association of India in 1926. It incorporates The National Council of Churches Catholic Association of India & Community for apostolate of catholic bishops' conference of India. It is a BORDERLESS fellowship of doctors, nurses, administrators, chaplains and allied health professionals. It is a potent instrument needed to bring about social reforms that involves mentoring Leaders, engaging in consultancy services and policy advocacy, interacting with church on health healing and wholeness, and supporting new health and development initiatives.

As the Church, we can be a source of strength and hope to people in distress. As the parable of lost sheep narrates, our good Shepherd mandates us to join Him to search, find and give new hope to our distressed sheep. I request each of us to join in this venture to make the services of this borderless Association known and to acknowledge God as the source of every healing.

Human Knowledge

Human knowledge has expanded immensely. Knowledge regarding human system has expanded beyond imagination. Cross cultural learning and strategic alliances in the field of medicine has made it an efficient instrument. I, being a gynaecologist, hardly understand what my son, a neurologist diagnosis or prescribes. The continued medical education gives us a glimpse of another speciality. Gone are the days when doctors like my father did cataract splenectomy and Caesarean section!

Disease do not have borders. Specially with availability of easy travel, disease confined to one region of the world can reach other regions. We had a taste of this during the recent Nipa virus epidemic in Calicut. The source of infection was traced to bats in a well. Two brothers cleaned the well, both got fever, went to local primary health centre where they were admitted. A nurse named Lene took care of them. Both got worse and were taken to a private hospital in Calicut.

The doctors suspected Nipa; blood samples were sent to virologist in Manipal. Nipa was confirmed. By this time, the two brothers succumbed to the infection. Nurse Lene wrote a farewell letter to her husband before she died. Then the whole medical system and government health services came into prompt action. Contacts were identified and isolated. The care takers used gloves and masks. Hand washing was taught to the public. Our cultural hobby of visiting the sick was restricted. In a months' time, the spread was curbed. Although by then, thirteen lives were lost.

We the servants of God who is the healer of the world must spread our network in such a manner that it covers all, just like the sunshine or the rain. Talking of rains, the recent floods in Kerala with its devastating effect and destruction has made the people of Kerala BORDERLESS. When bridges vanished, roads disappeared and houses were buried under water or soil due to landslides, all were called by a single name - homeless or displaced.

People lived in common shelters, school buildings, masjids, church halls and likewise. People from less affected areas, nearby states like Chennai, Karnataka, Maharashtra were sending help in form of food items, clothes and daily needs. This disaster has made the people borderless. It reminds us of the first Christian community where all the goods were pooled and shared (Acts 4:32-34). If a brother or sister is poorly clothed and lack daily food and one of says to them, "Go in peace, be warmed and filled "without giving them things needed for the body what good is that (James 2:15-16).

Medical Mission Enterprise

Any mission organised by church in connection with medical mission has to do with health, healing and harmony. In pure Heath model, the body is viewed as a machine to be fixed when broken. It does not consider the social aspect. In holistic model, positive health is emphasised. Health, according to WHO definition, is a state of complete physical, mental and social well-being and not merely the absence of disease. In wellness model, the ability of individuals, families, groups to cope successfully in face of significant adversity or risk is applied. Ecological definition is a state in which humans and all lives can coexist peacefully.

As a church community we must investigate each of these aspects. Each one of us can participate in one or other aspect of healthcare according to our capacity gift and talents. Preaching is essential, teaching is important, being a good neighbour is good, an environmentalist is needed, being a good homemaker is the need of the day. The underlying truth in all this is to be "Christ- like". We must reflect Christ in all our enterprise. It is said that we need drugs apparently because we have lost each other. In joint families, we had senior members to support and guide. Nowadays, when a baby has fever, we get upset; when wife goes into labour, the husband panics; when husband has chest pain, the wife crumbles. Due to flat system, we don't have neighbours; our contacts are in our mobiles. If it is not charged, we are lost.

Winston Churchill said, *"healthy citizens are the greatest asset any country can have"; this* applies to the church as well. When health is absent, wisdom cannot reveal itself, art cannot manifest, strength cannot fight, wealth becomes useless and intelligence cannot be applied.

This picture depicts an episode from my childhood. My father Dr. Cecil Macaden was a doctor in Jalna mission hospital in Marathwada for 32 years. He used to visit people on his bicycle. We never had a car but we, as family, always travelled in car which our friends lend. All of us were studying in hostel then. When we came home, my mother was an excellent cook and sometimes, hindu friends would send delicacies, muslim friends would send meat recipes, store person would send maida, the butcher's wife would bring liver, brain etc on Sunday. All these were shared for free for the love they had for my father. In this picture, I was about ten years old. My father had a heart problem on 25th December night. I woke up in the morning to see house compound and the main road full of people. They stood there for three days fasting and praying for my father's health. Surely this was a borderless experience.

So, live each day as if it was your last day. This would humble us; it will prevent us from hoarding. Be prepared to meet your Lord each day. When life is simple, the needs are basic. Where richness lies in the mind, we can follow where He leads. There are no borders to restrict.

"One day at a time sweet Jesus, that's all I am asking from you.
Just give me the strength to do everything that I have to do".

17

Rethinking Healing of Mind-the Role of Ecclesia as Being and Becoming Borderless Church:
Pastoral Care and Counselling Perspective

JM Sharath Sowseelya

Healing ministry is in fact an integral component of mission of the Church. The Church from the beginning has been contributing to the cause of healing in several ways. It's not a commencing effort but already existing one. However, the confessing fact is that Church has not been considered psychological problem and of its treatment as serious as considering the physical ailments. Perhaps the conventional interpretation of Texts related to psychological concerns confined to traditional healing methods and instigated stigma. Subsequently, somatic health has come to be the priority of the Church while the psychological well-being has not been emphasised as somatic well-being.

On the other hand, in the present-day context the psychological problems are as vivid as somatic concerns. A study conducted by the World Health Organisation in 2015 demonstrates that one in five Indians suffers from psychological concerns. The socio, religious, economic and global context is instigating numerous psychological problems such as behavioural disorders, trauma (e.g. PTSD), anxiety disorders, schizophrenia, dissociation, depression, phobias, panic attacks, suicidal tendency, insomnia, guilt, depression, anger, stress, low self-esteem etc.,

A quantitative study of National Mental Health Survey of India 2015-2016 identified a few common reasons for psychological disorders in India; they are- deprivation, poverty and unemployment, discrimination and abuse, social change and migration, stress and separation etc. Therefore, in this context, the Church being a border less community has two significant tasks, one is extending her borders for the cause of psychological well-being since healing psychological concerns as important as healing somatic ailments and another is healing the context that causes psychological disorders because most of the psychological problems are constructed in the cultural context of India. So, this paper explores the psychological and ecclesial (as a healing community) understanding of mind (psyche) and mental (psychological) illness. Also, explores the limitations (borders) and advances of the ecclesia as being and becoming borderless community in addressing psychological well-being. Finally, proposes strategies and implications for the Church.

Mind-Mental Illness- Healing: Psychological and Ecclesial Perception

Mind:

The mind is a set of cognitive abilities including consciousness, perception, thinking, judgement, language and memory. It is usually defined as the ability of an entity's thoughts and consciousness. Mind also referred as psyche/soul which is the totality of human consciousness and unconsciousness.

Mental Illness and Well-Being

Mental illness refers to a variety of enduring or recurrent disturbances in patterns of an individual's thinking, mood or behaviour that are typically associated with painful distress and/or impairment of social, occupational, or leisure functioning. Severity of symptoms may range from mild annoyance to extreme discomfort, from little or no violation of conventional norms to deviant behaviours, and from minor distortions of reality to significant impairment in behaviour.

On the other hand, mental health is a condition of well-being in relation to self and others characterised by such qualities as positive self-acceptance, accurate perception of others and the world, stability and appropriateness in mood, balance and purposiveness in her/his highest mental and psychological potentials. Thus, mental health is an active process not merely the absence of illness. The term metal health also connotes rehabilitation of mentally ill, prevention of mental and emotional disorders, and efforts to promote social-environmental conditions in which the individual can function according to reality testing.

Healing

R.A. Lambourne defines healing as 'a satisfactory response to a crisis made by group of people both individually and corporately, in simple terms 'restoration to a purposeful life.' New Webster's dictionary defines healing as wholeness, reconciliation and restoration.

Healing of Mind from Psychological Perspective:

The healing of the mind has been perennial concern of human societies throughout the centuries. In most ancient cultures psychological disorder was attributed to possession by supernatural spirits. Caregivers were usually priests or shaman-type religious functionaries who appease the Gods or exorcised demons. In some cultures, treatment was torturing the body of the individual. Healthy mindedness was assured by participation in religious rituals, observance of taboos, and the use of magical devices. With a few exceptions superstition and magic prevailed in the treatment of mental disorder. However, as medicine began to emerge as an art distinct from religion in classical Greece mental illness was increasingly attributed to natural causes.

The Naturalistic movement exercised considerable influence led by Hippocrates (460-375 BCE) and Galen (130-200 CE) who believed mental illness was imbalance among bodily hormones which affected the individual's brain. It was not until 18th century that medicine and the treatment of mental illness became stripped of supernaturalism and infused with the spirit of scientific inquiry and the treatment was placed in the hands of physicians. Under such leaders as Pinel, Tuke and Chiarugi, treatment became increasingly humane and optimistic. Many hospitals were built for treating psychological illness in Europe and America during that time, 1800s.

By the first decade of 20th century, psychiatry greatly aided by Kraepelin' system of classification had become firmly established as a specialty of medicine. At the same time Freud's revolutionary concepts about unconscious determinants of deviant behaviour and treatment by psychoanalysis slowly developed. Moreover, the two world wars brought vivid attention to the effects of stress and other socio-environmental factors on individual and community mental health. In 1950s the invention of antidepressant drugs and phenothiazine not only aided the treatment for many individuals with psychological concerns but set the stage for vital developments such as new advances in research regarding the neurological, genetic and biochemical factors that influence mental health and illness. Accordingly, many theoretical models have been advanced in efforts to organise the vast amounts of data about the mental health and illness into coherent explanatory frameworks and strategies for interventions. There are five theoretical models important today and the best treatment of medicines and therapies have been developed in order to help the individuals of psychological concerns. They are:

1. **Biological Model:** Genetic defects, bio-chemical imbalances, nutritional deficiencies and infections along with trauma, toxins and tumors etc. are believed to be the underlying causes of functional abnormalities in the central nervous system which appears to be associated with (many) psychological disorders. The developed interventions including chemotherapy, hospitalisation when needed, supportive therapy and electroconvulsive therapy etc.

2. **Psychodynamic Model:** Unconscious conflicts between desires and prohibitions are thought to generate anxiety which is defended against by various defense mechanisms. When defences prove unsuccessful the pathological conditions will occur. Therapeutic interventions are modifying behaviour by providing insights into relation between symptoms and underlying conflicts through exploring the client's dreams, and free association.

3. **Behavioural Model:** Pathological responses are perceived as learned responses. The problem behaviour is analysed based on its context and circumstances. Modification is affected through certain methods as desensitizing the client to problem producing stimuli with a stronger competing stimulus (muscle relaxation), new behaviour is acquired through various reinforcement techniques.

4. **Family Model:** The main source of dysfunction presented by 'identified patient' is said to be in family transactions. Treatment helps family members to communicate more clearly and openly, solve differences and achieve differentiation.

5. **Social and Community Model:** The principal source of (many) psychological problems is conceived as residing in the community. Treatment is geographically defined, and system focused.

However, no single model is universally applicable in all circumstances. In practise the helping person within the domain of his/her competence synthesises elements from those models that best fit the situation.

Healing of Mind from Ecclesial Perspective

The ecclesia is partially unsuccessful in adopting the development of medicine and psychiatry in understanding psychological disorders and well-being. From the beginning of the Biblical tradition, the psychological problem has been understood as possession by supernatural spirit. OT references to psychological problems include King Saul whose shifting moods, suspicious brooding and eventual suicide suggest a disabling psychosis, and King Nebuchadnezzar whose mind was made like that of beast and was dwelling with wild donkeys, a condition known in psychiatric terms as Lycanthropy, which are understood and interpreted in Christian tradition as demon act. On the other hand, mental deviation (madness and confusion of mind) is understood as Divine retribution for violating YHWH' commandments (Duet 28). The NT evidently presents psychological problems as demon possession and Jesus' is presented as a successful exorcist (Mk: 5:1-20, Lk 11:14, Mt 10:25, Mt 12:22f.) It is clear from the NT readings that exorcism was frequent and common in the early church and disciples continued exorcism as a part of mission commanded by Jesus. The present-day interpretations support the understanding of demon possession and exorcism promoting traditional expressions of healing such as anointing and charismatic and miraculous healing.

Healing of Mind (Treatment) - The Role of the Church

In fact, the medical doctors, psychiatrists, psychologists, clinical psychologists and trained social activists are the right people to treat and help the individuals of psychological disorders. The reason for that is that they are trained to classify disorders and to provide treatment accordingly in clinical terms.[1] The effective way of helping them is through pharmaceutical drugs, the method which is called pharmacotherapy. Certain cases do not require drugs but may need psychotherapy which includes several schools such as Gestalt therapy, Psychoanalysis, Cognitive Behavioural therapy, Rational Emotive Behaviour therapy, Eye Movement Desensitisation Reprocessing therapy, Group therapy etc., along with a few clinical techniques, muscle relaxation and meditation. Certain cases require both. Besides, individuals of all kinds of psychological disorders need care, advocacy, empathy and counselling and this is the point where the Church must extend her services.

The Role of the Church as a Healing Community

However, the Church must play a sensible role knowing her responsibilities and borders for the benefit of the individual. The paramount responsibility and role that the church can ensure is providing pastoral care and counselling. She got her own unique resources and strengths in providing PCC. The pastoral care and counselling is providing (healing)'wholeness' through five functions, healing, sustaining, guiding, reconciling and nurturing. Ultimately these five functions provide psychological support and caring. These five functions can be met through the utilisation of the unique resources of the Church including worship, Scripture, liturgy, literature, sacraments, rites and rituals, prayer etc.,

Christian worship is corporate in nature. Corporate worship contributes to positive mental health by providing an environment to experience a sense of belongingness, personal integration, diminishing of guilt and narcissism, reestablishment of a sense of trust, reconciliation, worthy of self-investment, and strength for handling her/his problems constructively. This corporate worship gives a strong sense of transcendence. The blending of horizontal (person to person) and vertical dimension (person to God) interaction gives the worship a unique ability to enhance mental well-being.

The religious resources have definite pastoral functions. Barnard (1981:350-351) identifies various functions of liturgy and liturgical singing such as lamentation, question and petition, belief and confession, liberation and joy etc., Prayer obviously one of the influential tools of PCC. It provides catharsis, trust on Divine and hope for meaning in suffering. Sacraments, rites and rituals offer reconciliation. Hence, each religious resource has a potential function in PCC. But the counsellor must be mindful that they are not the only instruments for healing the individual.

Strategies-Implications

A Paradigm of a Holistic Liberation-Growth of Pastoral Care and Counselling

Clinebell proposes a model of a holistic liberation-growth. This model is appropriate for the mission of the Church as a borderless church in the process of healing the psychological disorders.

- The primary goal of this model is to liberate, empower, nurture and wholeness centred in healing. This model perceives mind (psyche) as a unit of body, and spirit. Therefore, pastoral care and counselling must be holistic seeking to enable healing in all dimensions of human life.

- This model is systems-oriented, seeking the healing of individual as involving interactions among all their significant and interdependent relationships with persons, groups, institutions and of wider systems.

- This model enables people to increase the constructiveness of their behaviour as well as their feelings, attitudes and values.

- This model seeks to utilise and integrate both psychological and theological insights regarding the human situation and the healing of the persons.

- This model seeks healing by empowering the context and foundation of reparative ministry. Thus, it demands pastoral care (Church) to become more inclusive and to liberate herself from her own dominant structures (class, caste, colour, male orientation, traditional sex role stereotype etc.,). Therefore, the Church needs to strengthen her conceptual base and methodologies by drawing on the newer systems and healing-oriented psychotherapies.

- This model seeks healing to be occurred in all the diverse functions of ministry, including worship, preaching and social action. This also utilises unique professional identity and role of the minister.

Depending on this model a few proposed strategies:

- Socio-scientific approach to re-read and re-interpret the texts.

- An authentic Christian language of mental health from the sufferer's perspective ought to be developed rather than focusing on limited accounts of mental illness or demonic possession.

- Re-interpretation of accounts of Texts of mental illness and demonic possession in psychological terms. In the Biblical times the writers did not have medical awareness about mental illness and appropriate terminology to describe, hence they named mental illness as demon possession. Therefore, there is a need to reinterpret those Texts in psychological terms.

- A space must be provided for sufferers to find a Biblical and theological language to verbalise their own experiences which does not humiliate and marginalise them.

- A new theology of redemption and revitalisation needs to be developed as Biblical resources allow individuals to embrace medical science and to prevent the danger of 'over-spiritualisation'.

- A positive utilisation of religious resources. Avoiding the use of religious resources leading to self-pity and self-destruction. Also avoiding depending on religious resources alone for healing at the same time using healing potency of faith, grace, hope, and acceptance which is assured through the religious resources.

- Discouraging depending upon the traditional charismatic healing methods and encouraging to get medical, clinical and therapeutic help.

- Creating awareness of psychological well-being and disorders in psychological and clinical terms through workshops, seminars and preaching in order to ward off stigma towards and misconceptions about the psychological problems.

- Establishing hospitals exclusively of psychiatry.

- Appointing well qualified medical doctors, psychiatrists, clinical psychologists, counsellors and social activists.

- Getting the services of those medical and clinical professionals for the individuals at local level through conducting medical camps.

- Establishing counselling centres at local level and appointing trained counsellors and clinical psychologists.

- Establishing rehabilitation centres.

- Counselling and clinical training for clergy and chaplains, which has been known as Clinical Pastoral Education (CPE). The CPE is even more holistic, growth-centered, systems oriented, non-hierarchical, inclusive of the insights of feminism, humanism, and deeply rooted in pastoral identity.[2]

- Open to work with secular projects and NGOs, if it is needed.

- Introspection on how effective the existing healing ministry through hospitals, counselling centres, and rehabilitation centres (if at all already having this mission)

Referral counselling is a MUST if the problem is beyond the skills and borders of the Church.

Endnotes

[1] A valid and reliable classification of mental disorders is needed to ensure clarity in diagnosis and comparability in treatment. The authoritative resource for this purpose is-Revised third edition of Diagnostic and Statistical Manual of Mental Disorders of the American Psychiatric Association (DSM-R)

[2] In fact it is a pioneering contribution of Richard Cabot, Anton Boisen, Philip Guiles, and Russel Dicks. It was begun as training for seminary students and pastors as clinical counsellors and psychologists. It was on pathology orientation (an emphasis on diagnosis and treatment of illness). Later Carl Rogers contributed something of a balancing wholeness centeredness.

18

Church in Mothering Healing Relationships:

Insights from Attachment Theories

Livingstone Arputharaj

Relationships play a very important role in our personal development and social well-being. Our relationships influence and shape the world and people around us. In relationships we come to existence and are nurtured. We discover and define who we are and who others are in our interactions. They have a great impact on our social fabric. This behaviour to relate and to get attached is viewed by many psychologists and physiologists as an innate human behaviour for survival. Our human body is biologically designed to seek relationships. Our first moments of life begin with our preferential attention to the gestures and voices of others. Our neurophysiological and sensory filtering mechanisms enable us to focus on human contact and communication. Psychologists believe that certain relationships have greater impact on our life that they even determine the way we feel and think about ourselves, others and the world around us. Relationships that we experience have the potential to heal individuals and societies, to renew and rebuild a harmonious creation and to create a just and peaceful world. They can sustain individuals and communities even in times of extreme crisis. On the other hand, they can tear down individual and social wellbeing. They can erupt violence and abuse and can pose great threat to our very existence. Hence, it becomes important for us to nurture and develop relationship behaviours that are positive.

As a faith community, as Church, as followers of Christ, we are bound invariably by relationships. Our faith, our beliefs and our traditions are defined, nurtured and expressed by relationships. We are also commissioned to proclaim the good news of divine relationship that heals and brings life to humanity. We are also called to manifest this relationship that is founded on the love of Christ. Even as the Church of South India celebrates 70 years of its mission and ministry in a context where divisive forces are active in disturbing social harmony, pondering on 'Building Christ Communities: Towards a Borderless Church' is not only appropriate but dire need of the hour. To reflect on the above theme focusing on health, healing and harmony, I have tried to reflect on the importance of church being a community that becomes a source of healing relationships. I have used the framework of Attachment theory of John Bowlby to bring out how caregiving relationships can foster as well as destroy harmonious coexistence. Gathering insights from this theory, this article makes an effort to look at Church as a collective care giving communion and critically looks into its vocation to spread the love of Christ.

Attachment Theory: A Brief Outlook

Most of the psychological theories place great importance on human interactions and relationships; especially those belonging to the psychoanalytical tradition, emphasize the importance of the relationship between the primary care giver and the individual as something that has a lasting influence on the behaviour and personality of the individual. John Bowlby was the very first one to propose a theory of Attachment following which many have tried to substantiate it's claims with empirical proofs as well as some have extended and refined the theory through their studies. Bowlby's observations during his studies on children who were separated from their parents for a long period, motivated him to explore the bond created between the children and the primary care giver.[1]

Bowlby's attachment theory claims that attachments are part of survival mechanism in response to the human need for safety, security and protection. It serves as a biological function. Thus, for Bowlby, attachments are part and parcel of human evolution. According to Bowlby and Ainsworth, attachment is not mere dependence, rather a secure attachment will result in exploration and independence. A close relationship doesn't imply attachment bonds unless there is an attitude of seeking proximity and safety in times of danger. Bowlby studied on how the mothers who responded appropriately and sensitively to their children in times of distress helped them to develop a healthy attachment style. Bowlby in the initial formulation of his theory viewed attachment behaviour as something that is activated and then terminated based on need. But later he concluded that attachments are something that is active continually from cradle to grave.[2] The following section delineates the criteria that defines attachment bonds.

Criteria for Attachment Relationships

According to Attachment theory not all close relationships can be referred to as attachment relationship. Mary Ainsworth proposed the following criteria, meeting which the relationships can be claimed to be an attachment relationship.

Safe Haven: Mary Ainsworth observed that when children were alarmed by the feeling of being threatened or in danger, their anxiety level rises, and they immediately retreat back to their primary caregivers.[3] Once they feel pacified, they bounce back to normal behaviour. This very notion of considering an individual as a haven is one of the primary criteria of an attachment figure.

Secure Base: Secure base is the environment created by the attachment figure to the individual who seeks attachment. It provides the feeling of security that the individual needs to explore the world outside. Mary Ainsworth observed that infants use their attachment figure as a secure base from which they explore their environment by giving them a sense of confidence and safety.[4] This establishment of a secure base helps children to be more exploratory, independent and autonomous.[5] The secure base feeling helps an individual to take risks in life to attain his or her ambitions and goals.

Proximity Seeking: The individual has an innate tendency to maintain proximity with the primary care giver. The individual makes sure that it is in physical contact or to certain extent physically close with the attachment figure. They also show a great level of distress when separated from the attachment figure.

Separation Distress: When the individual is separated from the attachment figure, they show a great level of distress. They show certain level of resistance and protest to such separation from the attachment figure.

Attachment Styles

Mary Ainsworth in her observation of Child reaction to the separation of primary care giver concluded that child exhibit certain behaviours that were consistent with the proposal of John Bowlby. She also found that there existed a strong correlation between these behaviours and the attitudes of the primary caregivers toward the children in their caregiving interactions. She classified the attachment behaviours into three basic patterns secure, insecure-ambivalent and insecure-avoidant. The behaviours that were highly inconsistent were classified as insecure-disorganised.

Secure Attachments: In a secure attachment, the primary care giver can accurately sense the needs and attends consistently to the needs of the individual through predictable, prompt, appropriate responses.

In all the interactions, the perspective of the receiver is kept in mind. The interactions convey single messages that are consistent and not contradictory. Enough space is given to express feelings and the expressed feelings are acknowledged. There is fairness, openness, genuineness, warmth and empathy in the responses of the care giver. Individuals who experience such care environment seem to develop a very secure attachment style. They can handle uncertainties and ambiguities in life with very less anxiety. Such a secure environment allows the individual to be more explorative and independent. They can strike a balance between proximity seeking and exploration. On encountering fear or threat in their process of exploration, they can seek proximity of the primary care giver, they get soothed and continue their process of exploration. They can trust and depend on other with less fear of rejection. They show a greater level of intimacy, commitment and show positive attitudes towards their interactions. They see diversities and differences as something to be explored and understood rather than a threat for their existence.

Ambivalent Insecure Attachments: When the primary care giver is highly inconsistent, unpredictable in the responses to the needs of the individual develops a feeling of insecurity and anxiety. The care giver shows alternate unpredictable responses of care and rejection. They seem to care very less about the feelings and perspectives of the children rather are driven by their own self-centred needs.

The child learns that affection and care are unpredictable and can be attained only with great effort. It learns to give an exaggerated importance to the proximity of the care giver in order to reduce the anxiety. They begin to engage in activities that desperately tries to draw the attention of the care giver. Since the child is always preoccupied in drawing the attention of the care giver, it becomes limited in its explorative activities. This preoccupation gives rise to possessive and jealous behaviours in their relationships. They become dependent, rarely take risks and challenges in life. There is less verbal interaction that helps to express and understand the feelings and perceptions in such attachments. Often their sense of insecurity is expressed either as an exaggerated defensive expressions or suppression of expressions.[6]

Avoidant Insecure Attachment: When the primary care giver is consistently non responsive and insensitive to the needs of the individual, the child tends to display an avoidant attachment. The distress and needs of the children annoy and agitates the caregiver. In order to control such behaviours, the care giver express a dominating and controlling behaviour. Despite protesting and pleading for attention, when the individual is constantly subjected to domination and rejection by the attachment figure, avoidance is developed as a coping strategy.[7] They learn to limit their expressions of attachment need so that they avoid the pain of further rejection. They become self-reliant and more focused on exploration. This self-reliance and independence is an outcome of their fear of abandonment. They tend to see interactions as interferences and controlling very similar like that of their care giver.

Disorganised Insecure Attachment: When the very person from whom the child seeks safety and security becomes a source of abuse and threat, then individual is caught up in a complex situation unable to find ways and means to maintain an amicable relationship with the care giver. The care givers themselves are disengaged, hostile and confrontational. Such seriously difficult care environments push the individual to acute distress and disassociation. Since their repeated efforts to seek proximity and security ends up in failure, they become disoriented in their behaviours and interactions. The attachment figure itself becomes a source of distress.[8]

Care Giving Relationships and Formation of Inner Working Models

The attachment styles and relationship interactions of a child with the primary care giver constantly reinforce mental structures in an individual. A set of beliefs, rules and expectations about oneself, about others and the world is formed as a result of the relationship experiences.[9]They a play a major role in defining one's relationship behaviour and interactions styles. Bowlby called these as working models of attachment. These inner working models that are constructed by the child become the basis on which it builds further interactions. They also regulate the way in which emotions, attitudes and behaviours are expressed in relationships.[10]Even though these constructs are resistant to change, they are not completely static. According to Bowlby, though the initial relationship experiences have a strong impact in the formation of working models, these models are constantly reconstructed as the individual encounters new experiences. However, change in working models takes place at a very slow pace and are rare in their occurrence. [11]

From our childhood, we learn about ourselves and others from the experiences of interactions and relationships. According to attachment theory, the relationship that we experience with our primary caregiver becomes vital in this learning process. When there is congruence and consistency in the expressions of the primary caregiver, then the individual can experience and also form coherent relationship patterns without discrepancies. This leads to the formation of a healthy and secure attachment representations. On the other hand, incongruence in the linguistic expressions and the actual experience of relationships will lead to formation of distorted, unhealthy and insecure attachment representations.[12]

A securely attached individual will be having an internal working model that sees the care giver as a trustworthy and loving person and appreciates oneself as lovable and it extends this same perception towards other relationships. Conversely, an insecurely ambivalently attached child may view the world as an insensitive place in which people are unpredictable in their expression of love and affection and sees oneself as ineffective and unworthy of love. An avoidantly attached individual might feel unloved but is self-reliant. It considers the world and others as a interfering and rejecting. An individual with disorganised attachment pattern will have confused understanding of one self which is mostly negative as well as views others and the world as highly insecure and frightening. [13] According to Bowlby, these cognitive perceptions that are formed due to the childhood experiences of the care giving environment becomes the frame of reference for all the interactions throughout life span. However, these cognitive models are not completely impervious and does undergo changes though rarely and slowly, as one encounters new relationship experiences in life.

Attachment Patterns among Social Groups

Bowlby also recognized the role of social groups in acting as a care giver providing a sense of protection and security for human beings.[14] Social groups in human history has offered protection, nurture and emotional security to their group members. Antigonos cites the researches done by Smith and others which have empirically proved the fact that attachment styles with social groups have an impact in individual's interpersonal relationships. The attachment styles that individuals exhibited with the social group seemed to impact their relationship within the members of the social group as well as with the members of other social groups. Members who are anxiously attached tend to seek approval of others, extremely sensitive to criticisms and rejections and they also tend to see interactions with other group members as threatening. Those who are avoidantly attached to the group were more independent, less collaborative and tend to look down other group members.[15]

According to Antigonos, though in a social group, individual relate to one another within the group, the binding factor is often the social group, as a whole. The attachments established in the context of a social group is beyond mere interpersonal relationships. The attachments are established with the beliefs, values, traditions and practices associated with the social institution.[16]

Church as a Collective Attachment System: Relationship Patterns of Faith Communities

Church as social group in its true sense is a network of complex attachments. The relationship that exists within the faith community is not merely the relationships between its individual members. Rather, it is one that manifests as attachments with doctrines, beliefs, practices, morality and associated behaviours. It is also influenced by the historical experiences of faith community. These historical memories are interpreted by the community in their contexts to give new meanings that are relevant to their present experiences. Such interpretations are constructed individually as well as collectively and they redefine the attachment frameworks. Thus, construction and reconstruction of attachment frameworks becomes an ongoing phenomenon of the faith community. The cultural contexts of the faith community also have a major influence in its representation. These interpretative frameworks are used by the collective system to define, understand and interpret the human feelings, behaviours and needs both at a collective and individual level.[17]

Each Individual member becomes co constructors of faith, perceptions of God and relationships with the larger faith community. Despite diverse individual experiences, there prevails a common framework of collective representations that guide the attachments. In reality, each member of the body of Christ becomes a care giver expressing genuine care as well as a care receiver. The presence of such complex symbioses makes church a dynamic and powerful attachment system that can shape and alter human behaviour and thereby human structures. Church as an attachment figure seem to fulfil all the attachment criteria proposed by Ainsworth regarding the relationship characteristics between an attachment figure and the individual.

Church as a Safe Haven: Often the Church as a faith community is sought by its members as a haven in times of distress and danger. It offers channels through which one feels divine comfort and divine presence in times of inner struggle and external distress. Also, it provides a cohesive fellowship that provides emotional strength and comfort. Antigonos point out that researches show that people who have gone through loss and suffering have shown greater attachment with the members of the faith community as well as an increase in church attendance was also observed.[18]

Church as a secure base: Faith community creates an environment where one feels safe and secure not only in times of distress but also when no threat is present. Often people who are stressed by their mechanical weekly routines retreat to the fellowships of the faith community to be renewed and refreshed. For many, worships is seen as something that strengthens them to get back into the world that awaits with risks and challenges. People see church as a place where they can freely vent out the burdens of their heart.

Church and Proximity Seeking: We make sure that we are in constant relationship with fellow members of faith community. Church in many ways helps its members to feel the closeness to God through its ministry of the word, sacraments, prayers and other rites and rituals. Church also provides a spiritual space to experience the closeness and presence of God. It is through pastoral care and fellowship gatherings, relationships are nurtured and strengthened. Fellowship is one of the primary expressions of Church from its inception. It offers means to remain in fellowship with God and fellowship with one another. It helps us to gain a sense of belongingness and closeness which forms the vital characteristics of the faith community.

Church and Separation Distress: Any disruption in the fellowship affects our emotional and spiritual well-being and causes distress. Any such sense of disruption leads to guilt feeling that is resolved in confession and reconciliation.

Thus, we see that Church as a Collective system seem to meet all the necessary criteria to deem it as an attachment figure.

Relationship Approaches of Church as an Attachment Figure

Being a complex collective attachment system, Church houses systems that perpetuate healthy relationship styles as well as unhealthy and insecure relationship styles. Often in the history, faith communities have reached its low when it has been dominated by the perpetuation of insecure relationships, relationships that perpetuated individualism and self-centred piety and corruption. Despite such declining moments, the emergence of transformation in the form of protest and resistance against the existing system are witnesses of the healthy patterns perpetuated by genuine and congruent relationship styles. These relationships responded to the plight of the common, practiced what they believed and proclaimed and made efforts to make gospel relevant to the entire creation of God. At any given moment, faith communities are influenced by the dynamic forces of both insecure and secure relationship styles. And every moment provides opportunities for us to transform and move forward as a covenant community.

In the scripture we see this dynamic in the history of people of God. When the faith community is dominated by corruption, injustice and relationships that are abusive and discriminative, the prophetic community emerged as an alternate form resisting and protesting the existing immoral strands in the fabric of the faith community. They become agents of transformation even as they bear witness to this alternate life styles. Jesus movement is a transforming model that protested the then unhealthy systems of interactions that perpetuated insecurity and abuse among the faith communities. It challenged the attitudes that were towards possession of power and maintaining status quo at the cost of exploiting others and perpetuated alternate attitudes of relationships that motivated to love others as oneself. These alternative attitudes called people to be sensitive to the needs

and challenges of the least in the community. They reinterpreted
faith and God's blessing in the light of collective wellbeing as against
accumulation of wealth and power. They demanded everyone to
respect and treat others with dignity and value transcending human
barriers of gender, religion and race. These relationships were pathways
to see God in this earth.

Church in being and becoming an Exclusive and Unhealthy Structure

Church as faith community is ever prone to the danger of perpetuating
insecure relationships that destroy its very own commitment and call
to be a convent community of love. There were instances in the history,
where in the name of defending ideologies and status quo, church has
turned a blind eye to the cries of the creation of God and has alienated
and annihilated individuals and groups. It has perpetuated hostility,
violence and discrimination due to its misconceptions and spiritual
arrogance. Church as a collective community can be a perpetrator of
such unhealthy and destructive relationship attitudes that can hinder
its own wellbeing as well as the wellbeing of God's creation when
its ideologies and beliefs as well as its individual members exhibit
following traits of relationships.

- When Church refuses to see the signs of the times, the needs
  of the individual and the society and tries to impose its own
  perception of care and spirituality.

- When Church continually holds on to its oppressive traditions
  and refuses to collectively deconstruct and reconstruct their
  ideologies, beliefs and practices.

- When it teaches and preaches about love and compassion on the
  one hand but is hostile towards those who do not confirm to its
  beliefs and doctrines.

- When its teachings on one hand emphasize seeing the Image of God in all and on the other hand it discriminates people based on their gender, religion, caste and sexual expressions.

- When the collective interpretations of scripture and perceptions of God are dominated by the experiences of a few powerful to defend their status and comforts while the experiences of the culturally socially diverse communities are suppressed, marginalized and ignored.

- When the dominant perceptions of faith, belief and traditions tries to suppress the voices of dissent by judging and condemning them as sin.

- When there is excessive preoccupation to establish uniqueness and identity of the Church as against other social groups and essential values and principles are overlooked.

When Church structures and its individual members are influenced by the above ways of functioning and attitudes, then it becomes an exclusive, dominant and possessive community that fails to manifest the values of 'Reign of God' for which it is called to exist.

Borderless Church: Being and Becoming a Source of Healing Relationships

Church as a collective faith community, always encases the leaven of hope and transformation within itself in some form or the other. Despite all the challenges and conflicts within and without, it is a symbol of God's healing presence and God's just reign in this earth. God acts in and through the faith community to heal and transform the earth. Church constantly engages in the process of transforming itself as well as the world. Throughout history, it has ascertained its vocation to heal and transform itself and the world. As a collective community of fellowship, Church becomes a source of healing relationship as it continuous to exhibit and manifest the following characteristics.

- When church provides space for diverse expressions without suppression and engages in dialogues and is open to deconstruct and reconstruct its standpoints as followers of Christ.

- When experiences and needs of each member of the body of Christ is consistently acknowledged and attended.

- When church makes its bold expressions against injustice and exploitations and is willing to take risks for its call to establish the reign of God.

- When church enables communities to speak the language of love

When our individual and collective behaviours reflect the above prophetic inclusiveness, it is then we begin to nurture healthy relationships. Psychologists believe that a child learns to communicate or learns to speak language not merely listening to the noises and voices around rather it is the quality of relationship and the care that they experience helps them to develop language. It is the consistent and congruent mission and ministry of Church and its expressions of compassion and empathy that enables its members to speak the language of love that was commanded by Jesus Christ. Church then becomes a source of healing relationships.

Church of South India in reflecting the Mothering Nature of God: 71 years of nurturing Communion

Even as we celebrate and cherish the journey of CSI for 70 years, we are once again reminded of the vision that was foundational it is formation. It was an extraordinary effort to transcend the divisive barriers of denominations and to boldly proclaim the very essence of gospel which is to be in communion with Christ and one another. K.C. Abraham in one of his articles 'CSI after sixty years' rightly points out that CSI is not a denomination rather it is a movement for unity. It is a movement that acknowledged the uniqueness of each tradition amidst the realisation of the need to coexist in the love of Christ. It is a movement where faith communities made themselves vulnerable to embrace one another with genuineness and openness. It is a movement where possessiveness and rigidness ebbed away to truly experience our existence in the body of Christ. Church in its true sense realised its presence in the world as a covenantal community. The very urge to unite together amidst diversities is an expression of confidence and hope. Church of South India has been a source of this renewed hope and is a tangible symbol of nurturing divine presence and relationship. In has taken bold steps to a great extent to counter the exclusive structures that discriminate its members in the name of caste, gender and other divisive forces. It has made its voice clear and consistent against social and political injustices. As a collective communion, it has provided a secure platform to proclaim the good news to the marginalised and the poor. It has given space to investigate scripture and traditions from the perspectives of the 'other' and has even to a large extent have continuously revisited its purpose and mission to be more inclusive. The ongoing consultations of rethinking Ecclesia in terms of becoming a borderless church itself is a demonstration of its empathetic nature that bends itself to incarnate into the lives of each one. It is in this act of journeying together, CSI as a faith community manifests itself as a source of healing relationships.

Even as we are reminded of our vision and our efforts as a faith community in being true to our founding vision, it also becomes necessary to acknowledge and work on the aspects that reflect insecurities and inconsistencies. One cannot deny the existence of power in the hands of few which is at times misused or abused. The issues of the medieval church seem to still linger in our church structures exposing our selfish and power mongering attitudes. As K.C. Abraham points out 'church reflects the inequalities and discriminatory practices of the society.' In spite of the challenges from within and without, we are still abounded with hope to transform and to be transformed because of our faith in Christ.

More than ever before, we live in a context of powerful dehumanising divisive forces. Barbed fences and virtual walls mercilessly refuse life for those who desperately gasp for survival, voices of dissents that cry for justice are crushed to silence by the powerful and the dominant expressions and ideologies which are justified and imposed. It is in such a context, the role of church in being and becoming the source of healing relationships becomes essential. It is called to be haven and a secure base for those who resist against the divisive forces. It is called to communicate the language of love in words and action.

Conclusion

Church stands as an extraordinary symbol of hope and healing in this broken world. Church is not constituted by individuals who are perfect in every sense of the word. Rather, we are a community with brokenness, limitations and wounds. Amidst the challenges, we are called to be wounded healers in bringing about reconciliation and peace in God's creation. As we introspect ourselves, as we cross milestones in our journey of salvation, we are once again reminded of the transformative potential that we as a faith community are gifted with. Our very own existence is a witness to God's continuous work of salvation in this world.

Endnotes

[1] Cited by David Howe, et al., *Attachment Theory, Child Maltreatment and Family Support. A Practice and Assessment Model* (Hampshire: MacMillan, 1999), 12.

[2] Cited by David Howe, *Attachment Across the Life Course: A Brief Introduction* (New York: Palgrave MacMillan, 2011), 55.

[3] Cited by Vivien Prior and Danya Glaser, *Understanding Attachment and Attachment Disorders: Theory, Evidence and Practice* (Philadelphia: Jessica Kingsley Publishers, 2006), 22.

[4] Cited by Vivien Prior and Danya Glaser, *Understanding Attachment and Attachment Disorders...*, 22.

⁵ Jeremy Holmes, *John Bowlby and Attachment Theory* (New York: Routledge, 1993), 70.

⁶ Antigonos Sochos, *Attachment Security and the Social World* (New York: Palgrave Macmillan, 2014), 19.

⁷ David Howe, et al., *Attachment Theory, Child Maltreatment and Family Support...*, 27.

⁸ David Howe, et al., *Attachment Theory, Child Maltreatment and Family Support...*, 29.

⁹ David Howe, et al., *Attachment Theory, Child Maltreatment and Family Support...*, 21.

¹⁰ David Howe, et al., *Attachment Theory, Child Maltreatment and Family Support....*, 22.

¹¹ Cited by Antigonos Sochos, *Attachment Security and the Social World ...*, 14.

¹²Antigonos Sochos, *Attachment Security and the Social World...*, 16.

¹³ David Howe, et al., *Attachment Theory, Child Maltreatment and Family Support...*, 25.

¹⁴ Antigonos Sochos, *Attachment Security and the Social World...*, 26.

¹⁵ Antigonos Sochos, *Attachment Security and the Social World...*, 29.

¹⁶ Antigonos Sochos, *Attachment Security and the Social World...*, 45.

¹⁷ Antigonos Sochos, *Attachment Security and the Social World...*, 73.

¹⁸ Antigonos Sochos, *Attachment Security and the Social World...*, 46.

19

The Healing of the Mind
in Today's Context:
Towards Reframing a Borderless Church

D. Sudheer Karunakar

Introduction

The 'universal plan of salvation' says Thomas Manickam is carried out by the people who are called out for this purpose and are known as the church. This gathering of believers or the church was established to build the kingdom of God and to encourage and motivate each other in this process. Unfortunately, the churches have become more community oriented and biased towards the people of other community group. The power rests with the majority and the minority community stays marginalized this is also true of the churches with Dalit majority. There are divisions among the Dalit Christians which hinder the proper functioning of the church. This disturbs mindset of the congregation there is the need to heal the mind and make them healthy in order to build the borderless church. This presentation will therefore deal with the issue of unhealthy mindset (caste discrimination among the Dalit Christians) and its impact on the church and congregations in Telangana.

1.   Case Study

Mr. Pullayya, aged 70 years, was a Madiga[1] Dalit Christian and member of a Church in Warangal rural area. Most of the committee members and even the Pastor belong to Mala[2] caste. Mr. Pullayya involved himself in all the Church activities like working for mission fields, raising funds for the Church, and by helping the clergy in various capacities. He was a retired government teacher of the primary school. He was the only Madiga Christian with a government job. He never desired to become a committee member in his entire life; rather he had served the Church voluntarily. After his retirement from government, some of the church members advised him to take the responsibility as a Pastorate committee member so that he could serve the community life of the Church in a better manner. Also it would affirm the dignity of Madiga representation in the committee. So he showed interest to become a member of the committee but Mala Christians in committee did not allow him to be part of committee. Due to pressure from the people and committee, Mala Pastor had no choice but to accept him into committee. For the first time Mr. Pullayya had become member of committee to represent Madiga Christians. In committee he was often silenced and treated secondarily while making important decisions of the church.

Committee had decided to build a Parsonage for the Pastor in the Church premises. Mr. Pullayya was a highest donor for the construction of Parsonage. Some Church members advised to put his name in the tablet made up of granite. Many Mala Christians opposed to include his name in the Name plate, even Mr. Pullayya himself rejected the idea to include his name. At last by recommendation of the most of the Madiga Christians his name was included in the Name plate. After opening ceremony of Parsonage, this Name plate was broken purposefully, and Mr. Pullayya was abused verbally by Mala Christians in the name of his caste. He was also threatened by Mala Christians inside the Church. This situation made him to question his own identity and faith as a Madiga Christian. He was mentally, psychologically, emotionally disturbed not because of the broken Name plate but to experience such an excruciating pain and sorrow inside the Church, especially from the Mala Christians. He had given his resignation letter to Pastor and left his village and joined the church in Warangal Town. Mr. Pullayya died after he came to Warangal, his family members wanted to bury him in the native village, where his fore-parents were also buried. So they brought his body to native village, but Mala Christians and Mala Pastor did not allow his body inside the church for the final rituals before burial. Even the burial place was separate for Mala Christians and Madiga Christians of the same Church in village. Mala Pastor did not conduct even the burial of Mr. Pullayya. Another Madiga Pastor was called to conduct his burial service.

2.   Analysis of the Case study

This case study is just an example out of hundreds of painful stories of Madiga Christians in Telangana State. Few questions of concern that rise from this case are: Why Caste is still a great priority for Dalit Christians inside the Church? Dalits and Dalit Christians often accuse higher caste people, but when are we going to bridge the gaps between sub castes of Dalits within Christianity. How does the church, through its 'Health and Healing for All' policy, realize the construction of borderless community? A. Maria Arul Raja argues on history of oppression under the caste system called 'Dalit experience of thrown away ness' to expose the depth of their roots of segregation for centuries[3].

Unless all sub castes of Dalits are equally respected as full human beings, we cannot affirm the healing and health of Dalits in a pluralistic context. We meditated on the theme 'Plurality' it comes from Morality, this leads us to Equality. Without Morality there is no Plurality and Equality. Dr. B.R. Ambedkar says, "Depressed Classes must ally themselves to have Unity".[4] According to John C.B. Webster

'Madigas and Malas both accused and looked down on each other'[5]. In Telangana state, Malas played dominion over Madigas for centuries. The same segregation continues inside the churches. Bible says 'there is neither Jew nor Greek, there is neither slave nor free, there is no male and female, for you are all one in Christ Jesus', (Galatians 3:28). Much other discrimination such as:

During worship time there are separate seating spaces inside the church. Some places Madigas are not allowed to sit on chairs. They cannot read the Bible lessons, they can't share chalice with Malas, and they cannot be part of church choir. In certain places even the burial place was denied to Madigas near to the existing grave of a Malas. In Committee very few Madigas are made members and thereby they cannot partake in decision making process. Even Some places very few Madigas are pastors. Some Madiga pastors are suspended and some resigned. What is the reason behind it? This depicts the discrimination in the name of caste. That's why Mahatma Gandhi says "I like your Christ; I don't like your Christians. Your Christians are unlike Christ. So that, every Christian must be like Christ. Otherwise, there is no meaning of Christianity.

3.   Psychological understanding

Discrimination refers to unjustifiable negative behavior towards a group or its members, where behavior is adjudged to include both actions towards, and judgments/decisions about, group members. Correll provides a very useful definition of discrimination as 'behavior directed towards category members that is consequential for their outcomes and that is directed towards them not because of any particular deservingness or reciprocity, but simply because they happen to be members of that category'. The notion of 'deservingness' is central to the expression and experience of discrimination. It is not an objectively defined criterion but one that has its roots in historical and present-day inequalities and societal norms.[6]

Another psychological theory postulated by Tajfel and Turner's social identity theory is that there is a need for every social group to create and maintain a positively valued social identity for which they hold on to their group for valued dimensions such as material and socio-economic advancement, religiosity, equality and social justice.

4.   Psychological Consequences

The caste victimization instills in them the feeling of victimhood derived from various discriminating acts like not allowing to express their thoughts or feelings before the high caste persons, not allowing to come up in life, and keeping them always at the lower status by creating the feeling of inferiority in the minds of the people by making them unhealthy and their overall living conditions pathetic in the society. They also experience emotional stress, anger and shock and the other reactions including depression, mental distress, loss of confidence and self-esteem and even disturbed changes in the sleeping patterns.

Mr. Pullaya was so active in his old age that he wanted to be someone who was productive and useful to the people, when that was not fulfilled, he felt stagnated and the feelings of interpersonal impoverishment crept.[7] Though Erickson applies this to the middle years, yet we find it applicable in case of Mr. Pullaya. As result of the humiliated feeling of being silenced and not heard upon Mr. Pullaya felt the rejection and left the church and town. This is a clear indication of social isolation and unhealthy treatment. This again indicates the Erikson's theory which states that when the virtue of intimacy is not met then an individual acquires the maladaptive behavior of isolating self from the societal engagements. There is a need to heal the mindset of congregation in the church.

5.   Sociological understanding

Casteism in Dalit Christian community is an abiding reality in areas such as marriage, dining, education, Pastorate and Council committees and leadership. Although the church knows that Madigas have been denied the constitutional privileges and safeguards that are given in the name Dalits, because they are Christians, yet it refrains from helping them. Because of this a great majority of Madiga Christians are illiterate and are living below poverty line. Instead of helping the poor and needy Madigas, the church spends more money on conversions, which will help to strengthen its roots and at the same time ensures that the Madigas never rise from their level. Welfare of Madigas has never been an agenda for church, but a tool for the expansion of the church empire in India.

Conflict does not simply mean violence, but it focuses on the process of tension, disagreements, competition, and opposing view point on goals and values. These are the permanent and un-avoidable features of social life, and indeed an important source of change.[8] These symptoms are found in the case presented as both the Malas and Madigas were always competing and the tensions always existed between them. This shows poor health of the Madiga congregation because of unhealthy mindset of congregation.

6.   Theological Understanding of the Church

The gathering of believers is often called as the church. The Greek term '*Ekklesia*'[9] is translated as Assembly (Acts 19:32) or 'gathering' for some particular purposes.[10] M. M. Thomas seems to be in agreement with Chenchiah's idea of the church as an open Church should be open to the realities of the world and also it should be open to the world in cooperating and participating with Christ in respect of delivering the people from oppression. K. C. Abraham says that the Church has failed in reaching out to the people of all faiths and cultures and to act as a tool to witness Christ. S. J. Samartha emphasizes that the Church should transform the society by its action and deeds in order to draw the people of other faiths to Christ.[11] The Church seems to be reformed in principles but in practicality it has a long way to go especially with regards to the Dalits in the church.

7.   Present context of the church

Churches today are affected and driven by the materialistic values of our society. They followed the standards of the secular world – the bigger the better. So, they aim to build mega churches. Often, they justify their motive by saying that God wants their churches to grow. So, they work hard to increase their membership by using any means to do so, whether spiritual and secular.[12]

8.   Need for rethinking Ecclesia the Healing of mind to reframe borderless church

In this context, the church needs rethinking the healing of minds to be reframed irrespective of caste, creed, and race discrimination. In book of Jonah we find that all people of Nineveh king and slaves came together wore sackcloth sat in ashes repenting. Here all are treated equally. God expected nation to be in this way. This is real Health and Healing of the mind of the church. And another text says, 'For in one Spirit we were all baptized into one body Jews or Greeks, slaves or free and all were made to drink of one Spirit', (I Corinthians 12:13).

Let us take an example of Kerala victims. When calamities occur, it reminds us the meaning of Equality, Morality, Unity and Solidarity. Now they are all equal living together, eating together, and drinking together so on. Now, will the victim look at Caste of the food provider? Will he reject if the provider is of another caste? Where has the caste gone now? What about creed now? What about region? These are all demolished. These things work out during bad circumstances only. Pity thing is that after rescue the people come back to their same past mindset.

9.   Inclusive Church

The Church is called to serve indigent in the society. Church is called to accept people from various sub castes and various regions and treat them as equals. There is also a need to encourage marriages between Mala Christians and Madiga Christians so that Casteism can be diluted.

Church should be an inclusive community to include everyone.

The church must not have any reservation of places and seats. The policy is anybody can be seated anywhere as he/she likes and not the basis of their community. There must be one cup from which the communion is served. The voices of the Madiga should be heard before making any major decisions in the church. They should feel free to express their views and opinions publicly. They should be encouraged to take up the leadership roles in the church like becoming pastors, committee members and so on. To expect Madiga Bishops in the dioceses are also a dream.

Conclusion

In our everyday life, we travel in bus, train, flight (economy, business or executive) and lodge at various hotels. We travel equally on one board in order to reach our destination. My point is even we travel together in bus, train, and flight so on irrespective of caste, creed, colour. Why don't we follow that kind of unity in our life journey? We are sojourners in the world; we must reach our destination to God. During this journey why do we quarrel each other in the name of caste. For example, during Noah time all Holy (Healthy mindset) living things in the world traveled one board that is ark of Noah and rest of the unhealthy mind living things destroyed by storm.

This paper is to affirm the Healthy Mind of Christians as full human beings and to make unhealthy mind of the Christian heal to build a borderless church. Although Christianity propagates equality and sister/brotherhood, it practices caste discrimination within the Dalit Christian community. Christian preaching and praxis should match, until then discrimination continues within Dalit Christians for generations. It's high time for rethinking the Healing of mind to be reframed as borderless church in order to accommodate the people from all the strata of life without any prejudice and treat them as equals.

Endnotes

[1] Madiga Dalits were professionally called *Chrmakarulu* (leather workers and drum beaters) their deity was *poshamma* and *yellamma*.

[2] Mala Dalits were professionally called *Yellollu* (guards of the villages, messengers) their deity (goddess) name was *Mallamma*.

[3] A. Maria Arul Raja, "Inner Powers with Emancipation Agenda: A Probe into Dalit Roots" in James Massey et al.,*Breaking Theoretical Grounds for Dalit Studies* (New Delhi: Centre for Dalit/Subaltern Studies,2006), 151-152.

[4] B R Ambedkar, *Swaraj and the Depressed Classes* (New Delhi: Critical Quest, 2010), 29.

[5] John C.B. Webster, *The Dalit Christians: A History* (Delhi: ISPCK, 2009), 35.

[6] Correll, J., Judd, C.M., Park, B. and Wittenbrink, B. *'Measuring prejudice, stereotypes and discrimination'*. In J.F. Dovidio, M. Hewstone, P. Glick and V.M. Esses (eds.), *The Sage Handbook of Prejudice, Stereotyping, and Discrimination.* (CA: Thousand Oaks,Sage,2010). 84, 85.

[7] Barbara Engler, *Personality Theories* (Australia: Wadsworth, 2009), P. 159

[8] Palayam M. Balasundaram, *An Introduction to Sociology: A Study of Human Action and Interaction (Madras: MacMillan India Limited, 1981), 1.*

[9] Etymologically, the word *'ekklesia'* was derived from the verb *'ek-ekaleo'*, which meant 'to call people together' or 'to summon' them. Church is the gathering of believers with specific purposes with common goals. Paul greeted the believers of Colossians not as *ekklesia*, rather he addressed them as - 'the saints and faithful brothers and sisters in Christ', (Colossians 1:2). Mark D. Roberts, "*what is a church?*", www.patheos.com, (Accessed on 11-07-2017).

[10] Mark D. Roberts, "*what is a church?*", www.patheos.com, (Accessed on 11-07-2017).

[11] A. Vincent Thomas, *The Relevance of Latin American Church to Indian Ecclessiology* (Calcutta: R.N. Bhattacharya, 2000), p. 100-101.

[12] George Barna, *The Power of Vision* (Ventura CA: Regal Books, 1992), 34.

20

The Healing of the Mind in Today's Context: Towards a Borderless Church

A Historical and Theological Appraisal

Samuel Jayakumar

Make your tent bigger. Open your doors wide. Don't think small! ; Make your tent large and strong, because you will grow in all directions. Your children will take over many nations and live in the cities that were destroyed. Isaiah 54:2-3 (ERV) - ***On Wednesday, May 30, 1792, at Friar Lane Baptist Chapel,*** *Nottingham,* ***England, William Carey delivered an epoch-making sermon based on this text.***

"The religion of Christ is one of the most dynamic factors in the world. It always burst its boundaries, however strong and rigid those boundaries may be". V S Azariah, Bishop of Dornakal, (1932).

Introduction

This consultation is being held on the commemoration of the 500 years of Reformation, 70 years of CSI, Bicentenary of Serampore College (1818-2018), Centenary of the Senate of Serampore College

1918-2018). So, I quote the above two texts: one from William Carey, the father of modern India; and V. S. Azariah, the father of CSI and Ecumenical movement. Let us remember these texts as we read this paper.

I understand that the following are the questions asked in this consultation: how does the healing of mind enable border crossing? How are the expansion of human knowledge, cross cultural learnings, and strategic alliances in the field of psychology creating new alternative ideas and communities? How does the church, through its 'Health and Healing for all' policy, realise the construct of borderless communities? How has the church in its mission of healing enterprise already become borderless? Here the given theme is studied historically as well as theologically through selected case studies.

Our history and heritage

History is a diagnostic discipline; when studied it provides prescriptions for the present and for the future wellbeing. However, *"A sense of history is not natural to man. Societies have existed, and continued to exist, where there is little awareness of the ongoing historical process and no desire to find out what happened in the past"*.[1] Remembering and recalling the past is very important for every community. One can bring several illustrations from the history to illustrate the role played by the memory towards the reconciliation of races, religions and peoples.

I recognize that *"Rethinking the Healing of Mind in Today's Context towards a borderless Church" is* a relevant theme for this conference for various reasons. It is relevant because when in India Christians are falsely blamed and persecuted for promoting disunity, intolerance, etc[2] we have historical evidence to demonstrate that Christians always worked for harmony among the people and unity of the country including the unity of the people of the world and that is the way CSI was born. Apostle Thomas came to South India and preached the Gospel of peace;

Ebe Sunder Raj states,

> he came along the familiar trade route of the Arabs, Babylonians and the Romans. Thomas spread the redemptive message for twenty years in the kingdoms of Pahlava (of Gondophores in the Punjab) Chera Nadu (Kerala) and Mylapore (Tamil Nadu). The Indian Bhakti movement emerged after the time of Thoma and was impacted by the gospel. (vide Kural-Thuravu 350, the writings of the12 Alwars and the 63 Nayanmars"[3].

Then the Syrians, the Portuguese and finally the Protestants from all over the world came to this country with mixed purposes although the overriding aim was to give the Gospel to the natives of this country.[4] In South India commerce, civilization and Christianization all went hand in hand.[5] However, the overarching, undergirding and integrating aim was all could become children of one God, though the father of our Lord Jesus Christ.[6] That will in turn result in *one fold and one Shepherd* (John10:10).

Even so South Indians were the pioneers of the ecumenical movement. Inclusiveness is imbedded in the South Indian culture. For an example, *Yaadhum oore, yavarum kelir* had been the philosophy of the Dravidian south for the last two millennium or so. The proverb means, every place is yours and all are your people. This is a famous excerpt from Purananoor, anthology of poems during the third Sangam period of Tamil Nadu. (around 300 BCE to 300 CE.) From Tamil Sangam literature, it is clear that the South Indians were hospitable people. Section 9 of the Thirukural records several stanzas on entertaining the strangers and aliens by opening their hearts and homes.

Unlike other religions, the early Christian faith of South Indians' was not an exclusivinist way of life. The Early Indian Christians, especially of Apostle Thomas interacted freely with Saivaits,

Vaishnavites, Mahayana Budhists and Swatembara Janis and others.[7]
However, when theologically Christianity provided a critique of all
religions with an exclusive claim, it became therefore a basis for the
idea of the transcendental unity of all religions. As a result, all the
religions of India such as Budhism, Jainism, Vaishnavism, Saivism
are joined together and made one grand religion called Hinduism.[8]

Case One

V.S. Azariah, the first Indian Anglican Bishop (an ex-untouchable) and
a contemporary of M.K.Gandhi, B. R. Ambdedkar and J. W. Pickett,
has been considered as one of the invisible builders of the united
Republic of India, the world's largest democracy. In 1945, while the
British Raj was contemplating to appoint an Indian Viceroy, it was
mentioned about Azariah that, *"the only Indian who could possibly
carry the job of Viceroy is the Bishop of Dornakal, but the Government
would never have the sense to appoint him"*.

Bishop Azariah was modern India's most successful leader of
the Dalits solidarity and of non-Brahmin conversion movements to
the gospel of Christ during early twentieth century. His evangelistic
work among the Telugus resulted in enormous growth of Christian
congregations among different castes and communities resulting in
formation of a single united diocese comprising of all castes and classes.
He was consecrated Bishop of Dornakal in 1912, The first Indian to
become a Bishop of the Anglican Church of India.[9] The Cathedral that
he built reflects his dioceses' multiple ethnic and cultural traditions -
merging Muslim, Hindu and Christian architectural elements.

Bishop V.S. Azariah (a leader within one generation of the early
missionaries) understood mission as a common witness. It is not just
a witness of the single individual, but a witness of the whole church
to the whole world. He reported from his missionary experience that
the outcaste believers were a witness to the upper-caste non-Christians
outside the church. Thus, church could become an inclusive community

reconciled to one another. In other words, V S Azariah worked for a united church and unified nation. For him, Christian mission is both witness and journey within the world not a judgment made from outside. Mission is more of a journey than event just as history is a pilgrimage of the people. Mission is mission on the way – inviting people to take part in a journey that was initiated by our forefathers.

In the history of Christianity, the beginning of the Ecumenical Movement is the outgrowth of the missionary movement based in the southern parts of India. The historic World Missionary Conference that met at Edinburgh in1910 laid great emphasis on the need for united action and closer co-operation among the different missions and churches by crossing all kinds of borders and boundaries. The conference dealt with the question about the union of churches which also paved the way for co-operation among nations of the world. Missionary statesmen such as John R Mott, J.H Oldham and V S Azariah felt the need for harmony, peace - a greater union, not just the union of denominations, but union of nations that were warring in the early years of the 20th century.[10] In their opinion union of denominations and churches will result in political unity of the nations that would remove all kinds animosities. Mott saw the value of international Christian witness concerning issues of world peace and justice. Under his leadership, both the IMC and the YMCA engaged creatively in many partnerships with governments. In all these, Indian contributions were always present in the persons of V. S. Azariah, K T Paul and others.[11]

We must note that in the earlier days ecumenism was thus being discussed in practical dimensions by leaders such as John R Mott, J H Oldham[12] and others that lead to the formation of *League of Nations* that in turn resulted in establishing the *United Nations Organization* (UNO). In other words, in matters of unity, peace and harmony, the churches led the way.[13] In India missionary movement together with the reform movements resulted in national political unity and freedom.

The vision for unity and harmony was so pervasive so that it dreamt for greater union of churches in India: "So powerful is the hold of this vision on the CSI that in its very first synod (1948) there is a call for "wider unity".[14] The resolution reads: Fully persuaded as we are that such union is the will of God, and conscious that, that will cannot be fulfilled until all the separated members are gathered into one body, we, met together in the first synod of the church, issue this call to all other churches in South India to consider with us the possibility of a wider union".[15] The vision of a "wider union" of churches in South India was later enlarged to include the whole of India, with an occasional reference to the larger unity of human-kind. This is one of the major expectations of the CSI in the early decades.[16]

Soon individual leaders, groups and synods were deepening and enlarging the horizon of this unity asking such questions as: How far have we grown in unity? How far have we progressed towards being an Indian church? How adequately have we discharged our evangelistic responsibilities? [17] In 1992, when C.L. Furtado, then principal of the Karnataka theological College, addressed the synod, he said: The biblical vision of new humanity reconciled to God and re-integrated with God's creation should motivate us to move forward and to make the vision a reality. If the church is to be the sacrament of a new humanity, it must understand itself primarily as a community rather than as an institution or organization.[18]

On the eve of the jubilee celebrations, moderator Vasanth P. Dandin told the 1996 synod that "the visible unity of the major denominations was a partial fulfilment of the prayer of our Lord 'that they all may be one'. We have become one church, committed to the visible unity of the broken body of Christ."[19] Even so, Christian mission units not only Christians, but religions, peoples and nations. If so, as Ebe Sunder Raj has suggested, all independent Christian workers (if they prefer not to join a mission or a Church) should become part of an Association or Federation of similar ministries at State level or at National level in order to become interdependent, to give and receive and to become mutually accountable to one another. Unity without accountability is a misnomer".[20] This may or may not be possible, but this is one of the implications of crossing our borders and embracing others.

As another South Indian leader writes, we need unity, cooperation, networking and partnership among churches and missions. "We are used to the term 'unity,' and some churches have formed an organizational unity. But real collaboration and working together for a common cause is lacking. What we need is real urgency in focusing on common goals and working together to achieve them. Very often denominational and organizational barriers such as likes and dislikes of heads of institutions, doctrine, agendas of funding agencies, credit for success etc. come in for the lack of progress".[21] The need of the hour is networking and partnerships to demonstrate unity and harmony among ourselves – a visible demonstration of healing our wounds. Also, this will bring about synergy. We must maintain comity (cooperation, networking, partnership) in missions. Together we can achieve much more by synergy".

The nation is at crossroads today. Despite the economic developments, the nation is plagued by the pressing issues of corruption and immorality, intolerance and injustice, casteism and parochialism. We have a call to all God's people, particularly to Churches and Missions to come together, strategize together, work together in order to bring healing and wholeness to our land with biblical values and God's love.

Our Legacy of Healing and Reconciling, the Other

The church is an embodiment of health and healing. According to Clebsch and Jackle, *healing is a pastoral function that aims to overcome some impairment by restoring the person to wholeness and by leading him or her to advance beyond his or her previous condition. Thus, a pastor is a healer, physician and restorer. So also, reconciliation is another pastoral function. Reconciliation seeks to reestablish broken relationship between man and man and between human and God. Historically reconciling has employed two modes, that is forgiveness and discipline.* [22]

To be healer is to recognize and understand something of the source of another person's wounds. It isn't to be in the analysis-business, or to pretend to a professionalism which is superfluous. It isn't, either, so to concentrate on the wound that the wound becomes the person and its healer sees a problem and not a person. It is to give the wound space, time, air; it isn't to be ready to apply a miracle cure, or a magical adhesive plaster, or to take away the risk of scars. It is to allow the poison to seep out, and in so doing to be ready to absorb it. If bitterness has been allowed to drain away, scars can be valuable evidence of suffering experienced and transformed. Some wounds are of such long-standing, have cut so deep, that the poison has already done its lasting work; the job of the healer then becomes the job of the guider. Sometimes the wounds are hard to get at, because to avoid the hurt they cause us, we have pushed them hard away, thought they were too painful even to examine; we've found the memory too keen, or the guilt too hard to bear. But trying to forget, trying to act as though they never were, only makes wounds more poisonous still. And task of the healer we're called to be gently to help the other to recognize the hidden sore.[23]

Reconciling[24] which helps people to agree together, or be restored to friendship and fellowship, with God, with others, and often with their own feelings and desires. The relationship between God and humans is continually being broken and feelings of guilt, shame, and sorrow are real in people's lives. Personal relationships become twisted and torn through harsh words, actions, and attitudes. But broken relationships can be restored through acceptance and forgiveness, and new relationships can be formed[25].

To be a reconciler is not necessarily to be looking for the role of dramatic intermediary, or even that of the soft-footed go between. Of course, there may be times when we are called to be reconcilers in a practical way. We may have to receive the confidences of two people whose relationship has broken down; we may have to represent coolly and dispassionately to a third party someone else's grievances. We will then recognize that reconciliation isn't the business of modifying convictions or asking anyone else to do so; it isn't matter of speaking other than the truth to accommodate people or make circumstances easier.[26]

Case 2

Is it possible to truly forgive and forget the evils committed against us? This is the question of Miroslav Volf's 2006 work titled: *The End of Memory*.[27] Volf does not write theoretically about the complications of remembering violence rightly. He was interrogated for eight years by the Communist regime for being both a Christian and a "Western sympathizer". He writes with much reflection on his own story, using it at times as a lens to bring out the practical implications of his ethic. He explains challenges of "remembering rightly," and yet he still maintains that right remembering seeks to reconcile the offended and the offender. The grounds for such an ethic are the gospel of Jesus Christ.

Volf's book is divided into three parts. Part one explores the nature of remembering. He analyzes here the ways in which we can remember wrongs suffered. He speaks of memory as both a shield and a sword and using memory as a means of healing or using memory as a means of harming others. We can remember masochistically – in order to express displeasure with myself and my failures; or we can remember sadistically – in order to take revenge or repay evil on another; or we can remember Biblically – remembering in order to speak the truth and love the wrongdoer.

In part two, Volf turns his attention to the method of remembering rightly. He explores the challenges of remembering rightly and the framework needed in order to do so. Fundamentally we must acknowledge that the act of remembering is difficult in and of itself. Our finitude, the passage of time, and our own prejudice make remembering a complicated matter and often the whole truth can elude us. But remembering is a matter of justice.

> For when perpetrators "remember" untruthfully, their stories are a continuation of wrongful deeds in an altered form. They add the insult of misrepresentation to the injury of the original violation. And when victims "remember" untruthfully, their stories are often attacks on perpetuators in response to injuries suffered; they retaliate illicitly. To "remember" untruthfully is not only to continue but also to deepen in memory the conflict created by the initial injury. It is to add fuel to the fire of the already existing conflict. To remember truthfully, on the other hand, is to render justice both to the victim and to the perpetrator and therefore to take a step toward reconciliation.

There is a moral obligation to speak the truth; Christians know this as the obligation to speak the truth in love. The application of this principle requires us to both avoid the negative, not speaking falsely, and to enact the positive, to speak well of others. This means remembering is a "form of doing," it is an active response. We "use our memories" and therefore Christians must evaluate carefully how they are using their memories. We need, then, to evaluate the frameworks we use to make sense of our memories. The Bible presents us with both examples and a theological grid for remembering rightly. The gospel of grace and the promises of Christ become the lens through which we remember rightly. This is a hard truth, and many will find the book too difficult. After all, the very thought of doing justice to those who have violated us, wronged us, and performed injustice seems in and of itself to be wrong. Volf is not naive to these thoughts and to the emotional challenges of remembering violence. But it is the gospel that frames his ethic of remembrance, as such it is hard but right.

Part three turns attention to the question of longevity. "How long should we remember" is the question that unifies the remaining four chapters. Here he orients us towards the hope of reconciliation with the wrongdoer. He urges us to see that Christian faith insists on desiring reconciliation. Yet, he also humbly acknowledges that this is an element of life that probably awaits fulfillment in the Kingdom of God. The goal is to "forget," seeking to get to a place where the event of wrong no longer comes to mind. One can appreciate the challenge such a definition presents to reality, and yet Volf is ever optimistic that we can move towards this level of reconciliation, of true forgiving and forgetting.

Furthermore, Miroslav Volf's contributions to theology of reconciliation are noteworthy. In another book, *Exclusion and Embrace: A Theological Exploration of Identity, Otherness, and Reconciliation* provides an in depth look at a theology of reconciliation. [28] In *Exclusion and Embrace*, Miroslav Volf begins by laying a foundation for his case for reconciliation. He believes that the identity of persons and how they are to relate to the other ought to be determined by the model God has given humanity in the cross of Jesus Christ.

Applying the work of John Howard Yoder and Jurgen Moltmann, Volf argues that the work of reconciliation ought to be centered on the theme of "self-donation." This means that in the same way that God donates himself in Jesus on the cross for the sake of others, so also humanity should self-donate themselves for those that seem undeserving. Self-donation when understood as self-giving love is such that Christ "died for the ungodly" (Romans 5.6) so that those who were by nature evil and enemies of God, can find in the cross a reconciling embrace. Volf states later in the book: *"At the heart of the cross is Christ's stance of not letting the other remain an enemy and of creating space in himself for the offender to come in."*

Along with the open-arms of Jesus on the cross for his enemies, two other biblical images support Volf's case for self-donation. He cites the trinity as having an intricate self-giving love. Modeling the

Trinity gives us reasons to give of ourselves to the other. Also, a relevant image for reconciliation is that which is found in the story of the prodigal son. The father has an open posture of the will to embrace his estranged son. These three images form three doctrinal foundations for reconciliation: 1) the doctrine of God, 2) the doctrine of Christ, and 3) the doctrine of salvation. It is these three doctrines expressed by the above three images that give credence to the whole of his perspective on making room for those with whom we may have a conflict. In an interview he points to the following quotation from his book as the fundamental thesis of his theology of human reconciliation:

> The will to give ourselves to others and "welcome" them, to readjust our identities to make space for them, is prior to any judgment about others, except that of identifying them in their humanity. The will to embrace precedes any "truth" about others and any construction of their "justice." This will is absolutely indiscriminate and strictly immutable; it transcends the moral mapping of the social world into "good" and "evil.

Case 3

Desmond Tutu and the Truth Reconciliation Commission:

A year after the attainment of majority rule, Archbishop Desmond Tutu was appointed chairman of the TRC. Its jurisdiction included providing support and reparation to victims and their families and compiling a full and objective record of the effects of apartheid on South African society. Anybody who was a victim of violence was welcome to give his or her testimony before this newly constituted body. Perpetrators of violence could also give evidence and request amnesty from prosecution.[29]

The Government envisioned the TRC as a mechanism that would help deal with the evils of apartheid. In the words of the former Minister of Justice, Dullah Omar, the commission was "... *a necessary exercise to enable South Africans to come to terms with their past on a morally accepted basis and to advance the cause of reconciliation."* The application of the system of apartheid had led to the escalation of conflict in the country which resulted in violence and human rights abuses. No section of society escaped these abuses, but, to the South African government's credit, it was recognized that "to err is human but to forgive is divine." [30]

Forgiveness

The primary objective of the inquiry was to preach forgiveness in order to heal the emotions and wounds of hatred or anger that had been created by the apartheid system. There was no place for retaliation in the new society that emerged after independence. It was envisaged that "one who forgives becomes a better person than the one being consumed by anger and hatred." By the same token, it was also argued that "If you can find it in yourself to forgive then you are no longer chained to the perpetrator. You can move on, and you can even help the perpetrator to become a better person too." Nevertheless, the process of forgiveness also required acknowledgement on the part of the perpetrator that they have committed an offence. The Chairman of the Commission noted that he had actually "witnessed so many incredible people who, despite experiencing atrocity and tragedy, have come to a point in their lives where they are able to forgive." Take the Cradock Four, for example. "The police ambushed their car, killed them in the most gruesome manner, set their car alight" in the Eastern Cape in 1984. When, at a TRC hearing, the teenage daughter of one of the victims was asked: "would you be able to forgive the people who did this to you and your family?" She answered, "We would like to forgive, but we would just like to know who to forgive."[31] Let us give and forgive so that we will be healed, and others also will be healed.

Conclusion

We are living in an unexpected, but revolutionary century. The political ideals of liberal democracy seem to be failing, while the economic system based around financial capitalism is losing legitimacy fast. How might Christians respond? Certainly, we need the courage of the reformers, who turn to God and his Word for wisdom and direction for promoting God desired change. Indian reformer such as Jothirao Phule, B R Ambdedkar V S Azariah, E V R Periyar and others fought against Hindu fascism and communalism. As we are aware today new form of dangerous political leadership is emerging in different parts the world, particularly in our country. Although this is not the first, and likely not the last time, the threat today of what can be called the new fascism is real. As an ideology characterized by fundamentalist, militant, nationalistic, and racist policies, fascism threatens especially the "other," be it the poor, the oppressed, or the disenfranchised - people for whom God has a special concern. What the Seminary and the Church can do when we want to celebrate the 500 years Reformation and 70 years of CSI and 200 years of Serampore College.

Let us think about our legacy and returned to our roots – Let us love one another as we love ourselves. Let the Church in India demolish its borders so that we may be one. Let us remember Jesus' prayer found in John 17: 21 - *Father, I pray that all who believe in me can be one. You are in me and I am in you. I pray that they can also be one in us. Then the world will believe that you sent me.* Let us be truly Catholic in our personality with space for others. May the Lord give us enlarged hearts so that our Church will be enlarged, and the Word of God may increase and prevail.

Endnotes

[1] D. Bebbington, *Patterns in History*, (Leicester: Apollos, 1990), p.21.

[2] Jenkins has rightly observed, "fears that Christians might take even deeper inroads among the poorest go far towards explaining the recurrent persecutions and mob violence directed against the churches across India,

actions that often occur with the tacit acquiescence of local police and government. Matters have deteriorated sharply since 1997, when the Hindu nationalists enjoyed an electoral upsurge". See P.Jenkins, The Next Christendom: *The Coming of Global Christianity,* (Oxford: OUP, 2002), p.184

[3] Ebe Sunder Raj, "Our Land, Our Messengers, Our Mandate" in *Mission Mandate – NMC,* Chennai, MEB, 2018.

[4] S.Jayakumar, *Mission Reader,* Oxford Regnum, Delhi, ISPCK, 2002, p.130.

[5] Daniel O' Connor, *The Chaplains of the East India Company 1601 – 1658,* Continuum, 2012

[6] The Great Commission of Jesus Christ had a geographical dimension and we should remember that Christian mission carried out from that point of view has been one of the significantly contributory factors to the globalization process. It is true that great voyages were undertaken by the medieval European travellers not just for the sake of 'pepper trade' as historians have told us, but to propagate the Gospel of Christ. It was under the umbrella of world evangelisation that trade progressed and sea routes between the East and the West were discovered.

[7] The author of this paper has done a study on Dravidian religious traditions and his research is published. See chapter 2 in *Mission Reader,* Oxford, Regnum 2002.

[8] Ninian Smart, *Religion and Nationalism,* Delhi, Sat Guru Publication, 1994 p.34.

[9] For a detailed contribution of V.S. Azariah, see Susan Harper, *Under the Shadow of Mahatma,* Cambridge, Eerdmans, 1999.

[10] "Among the qualities most needed among those who aspire to true leadership in the fostering of peace and goodwill among the nations and in overcoming racial and religious antagonism is the cooperative spirit and objective. Elihu Root who ever illustrated this trait, emphasized the fact that you can measure the future greatness and influence of a nation by its ability to cooperate with other nations. John R Mott, From **Nobel Lectures**, *Peace 1926-1950,* Editor Frederick W. Haberman, Elsevier Publishing Company, Amsterdam, 1972.

[11] John R Mott Noble lecture, December 13, 1946. Kanakarayan Tiruselvam Paul (24 March 1876 – 11 April 1931) was the first Indian -born National General Secretary of the National Council of YMCAs of India. A Christian himself, he explored the relationship between Christianity and national identity. He held positions such as President of the Governing Council of the United Theological College, Bangalore, General Secretary of the National Missionary Society (India), and Chairman of the National Christian

Council of India. Paul's lasting legacy was rural reconstruction, which he initiated through the YMCA in India. He represented the Indian Christian Community at the first round table conference at London during 1930-31.

[12] Born of Scottish parents in India, Oldham graduated from Oxford in 1894, then served with the Young Men's Christian Association in India for three years before embarking on theological study in Edinburgh and Germany. In 1908 he was appointed organizing secretary for the epoch-making 1910 Edinburgh World Missionary Conference, and he was subsequently named secretary of the conference's continuation committee. Hopes for rapid advances in ecumenical cooperation among mission boards were set back by World War I, but the International Review of Missions, founded by Oldham in 1912, quickly became a most significant organ of research into missionary practice and theology on a world scale. He remained editor until 1927. Keith Clements. "Oldham, Joseph Houldsworth," in *Biographical Dictionary of Christian Missions*, ed. Gerald H. Anderson (New York: Macmillan,1998), 505-6

[13] John Nurser, *For All Peoples and All Nations : Christian Churches and Human Rights*, Geneva, WCC, 2005.

[14] S J Samartha, "Vision and Reality, Personal Reflection on CSI, 1947 – 1997..." *Ecumenical Review*, Oct 1997.

[15] Proceedings of the First Synod, March 1948, Madurai, p.5.

[16] S J Samartha, "Vision and Reality, Personal Reflection on CSI, 1947 – 1997..." *Ecumenical Review*, Oct 1997.

[17] R.D. Paul's report on the Nagercoil Synod (1958), in The First Ten Years, pp.3-7.

[18] Proceedings of the Twenty-third Synod, Palayamkottai, Jan. 1992, p.72.

[19] Cited in South India Churchman, special number on the synod, Coimbatore, 1996, p.1.

[20] Ebe Sunder Raj, "Our Land, Our Messengers, Our Mandate" in *Mission Mandate – NMC*, Chennai, MEB, 2018.

[21] R. Theodore Srinivasagam, Present Trends and Priorities in Today' in *Mission in Mission Mandate – NMC*, Chennai, MEB, 2018.

[22] According to Clebsch and Jackle there are four functions of pastor: Healing, Sustaining, Guiding, and Reconciling.

[23] Frank Wright, *Pastoral care for lay people* (London: SCM Press Ltd, 1982), 24.

[24] It is believed that by forgiveness and discipline, Reconciliation enable persons to gain deeper relationships with God and neighbor; c.f. J.F. Hopewell, "Pastor (Definition and Functions)" *Dictionary of Pastoral Care ...*, 827.

[25] Harold Taylor, *Tend my sheep...*, 32.

[26] Frank Wright, Pastoral care for lay people (London: SCM Press Ltd, 1982), 35.

[27] https://pastordaveonline.org/2018/02/26/a-review-of-the-end-of-memory-by-miroslav-volf/

[28] http://www.patheos.com/blogs/thepangeablog/articles/unpublished-papers/contextual-theologian-reflection-miroslav-volf/

[29] http://www.sahistory.org.za/article/tutu-and-his-role-truth-reconciliation-commission

[30] http://www.sahistory.org.za/article/tutu-and-his-role-truth-reconciliation-commission

[31] http://www.sahistory.org.za/article/tutu-and-his-role-truth-reconciliation-commission

21

A Psycho-theological Understanding of 'Atonement' and It's Relevance to the Healing of the Mind in Today's Context

Towards a Borderless Church

John Nischal Kumar

1. Introduction

The parable of unity is affirmed through the formation of the Church of South India by overcoming the borders of denominational faith, mission allegiance and regionalism. But still in this globalized era borders exist in the form of class, caste, gender, power, age, culture, home, family, congregation, faith communities, village, town, state, country and so on. Sometimes we struggle to share borders, cross borders and merge borders, yet borders do exist. At this point of time the call for a borderless Church is alarming. A borderless Church can be achieved through many procedures; one among such procedures deals with the psychological intervention. Psychological understanding of the theory of 'Atonement' acts a channel to deal with healing of the mind, thereby it guides us towards a borderless Church.

Atonement is "the state of being of becoming 'at one,' reconciled, with someone else."[1] In Old Testament times atonement refers to the sacrifice, sanctify, purify and so on. In New Testament times atonement refers to the person and work of Christ and death and resurrection of Christ. Christ's sacrificial act brought salvation to the humans and reconciliation between God and humans. Robert S. Paul quotes Webster's definition of the atonement as,

> A Satisfactory reparation for an offense or injury. That means the action of setting at one, or condition of being set at one, after discord of strife (the restoration of personal good relations wither by reconciliation or appeasement, reparation of wrong or injury).[2]

The theory of 'Atonement' is used as a lens to view the wider concept of, 'Healing of the mind in today's context towards a borderless Church.' Theological and Psychological perspectives of Atonement will enable us to widen our cognitive capacities and help us to formulate and adopt psychological sacrifices; this can direct us towards a borderless Church.

2.   Theological Understanding of Atonement

2.1. Old Testament Theology

The Atonement in Old Testament is basically Substitutionary idea which focuses on the practice of Sacrifice.[3] From the time of Adam the Substitutionary idea existed. When Adam and Eve disobeyed God's words they became sinners and the penalty for the sin is death (Gen3:19). After announcing judgment God made garments of skin for Adam and Eve (Gen 3:21). John M Brown says that, according to Henry M Morris:

> Perhaps they silently and sorrowfully watched as God selected two of their animal friends, probably two sheep, and slew them there, shedding the innocent blood before their eyes. They learned, in type, that an 'atonement' (or covering) could only be provided by God and through the shedding of blood on the altar.[4]

From this statement, we can understand that through sacrifice, sins are forgiven i.e., for the sins of humans, substitution was made through shedding the innocent blood. Here we can understand that *restoration of personal good relations is made by reconciliation* between God and Humans through the act of sacrifice. From then on, this concept was widely followed. During Patriarchal period Abraham and his descendents also followed Sacrifices. God provided an elaborate system of sacrifice during Moses time.[5]

The principle of substitution was shown in sin offerings.[6] From then on through the history of Israel in the Old Testament times the sacrifice became the substitutionary idea for the forgiveness of the sins. Later there was a slight shift arising during prophetic times that forgiveness does not merely comes from the external sacrifices, but God will be pleased with the inward cleansing and sacrifices of our heart. Prophet Isaiah brings out the concept of Suffering servant to show that righteous will suffer for many[7]. Prophet Micah also says that burnt offerings are not important but justice, love, kindness, humbleness is important.[8] J.K Mozley in his book, The Doctrine of the Atonement quotes Mr. Montefiore that, "the main doctrine of Judaism on the subject of atonement is comprised in the single word repentance, and under repentance was included and understood amendment."[9] He summarizes that the whole ceremony of sacrifice is for the confession of sin. Priestly tradition spoke about external sacrifices where as Prophetic tradition spoke about repentance. We can understand that in Old Testament times the *satisfactory reparation* (Sacrifice) is required when there is *discord or strife* (here in this context it is Sin). High Priests in Old Testament context acted as channels in *restoring reconciliation* between God and Humans through sacrifices.

2.2. New Testament Theology

During Jesus' time there was a strong continuation and emphasis on priestly tradition which focuses on external sacrifices. The prophetic tradition was ignored because it was hard to follow. Edward Grubb says that, "the prophetic religion had shriveled to Pharisaism, and had become in large measure legal, hard and cold."[10] John the Baptist and Jesus went on with prophetic tradition and never insisted on external sacrifices but called people to repent and live a righteous life. The prime question which arises is that, 'Is Jesus against Levitical law? J.Ramsey Michaels quotes few New Testament texts to explain this issue such as, Mark 8:31 says that, 'the son of Man must undergo great suffering...', Matthew 26: 28 says that, 'this is my blood of the covenant, which is poured out for many for the forgiveness of sins,' and says that,

> It is important to observe that Jesus does not stand against the law but views himself as the one who fulfills it in all aspects (Matthew 5:17-18). The atoning work of Yahweh in the Old Testament is exemplified in the shedding of blood for the remission of sin, by which he reveals that rebellion against him is deserving of death and that only by the divine principle of a life for a life is his demand for righteousness and justice satisfied.[11]

From here, we can say that the Jesus himself sacrificed for the human sins. The Gospels suggests us to repent and live according to the Divine love which is shown by Jesus on the cross.[12] Jesus fulfilled the atoning task of reconciling God and fallen humanity. Jesus' activity of releasing, reconciliation, restoration, propitiation and atonement shows the image of ruler, deliverer, guide, shepherd and so on.[13] Paul in all his Pauline epistles says that Jesus' suffered and sacrificed himself on the cross for the remission of sins. Gal 1:3, 4 says that, '... *the Lord Jesus Christ, who gave himself for our sins to set us free from the present evil age...*' The *satisfactory reparation* of sin is done by Jesus by sacrificing himself on the cross and thereby he restored *the good personal relations* between God and humans through reconciliation.

3. Psychological Understanding of Atonement

3.1. Understanding Atonement from the writings of various Psychologists

3.1.1. Sigmund Freud

Freud in his book 'Moses and Monotheism' speaks about renunciation and gratification. He says that Id is the aggressive nature of human nature and it is satisfied by the pleasure and demand. Id leads to the gratification. Ego on the other side helps an individual to renounce the gratification. Ego gives obedience and reality principle. Super-ego on the other side gives more emphasis on the criticism and prohibitions. The transcendence from Id to Ego and Super-ego to Ego gives the reward of morality and happiness.[14] This transcendence can be understood as the satisfactory reparation made to develop ego and thereby atonement in human nature is possible.

Freud's another famous work 'Totem and Taboo' also highlights that the acts of atonement are essential to restore the sanctity. Totem means it is a sacred symbol created by the group of people, it might be an animal or plant or rain or water or guardian spirit and so on. Totem clans' i.e who follows same totem need to live peacefully. Violation of such rules and regulation leads to the punishment.[15] The word Taboo used for sacred and forbidden or dangerous objects. Violation of taboo also leads to punishment. Freud says that, "certain of the dangers brought into existence by the violation may be averted by acts of atonement and purification."[16] The violation of the totem and taboo is a punishment and atonement need to do for restoring the sanctity.

3.1.2. Alfred Adler

The focus of Adler's personality theory is a "unitary, goal-directed creative self which in the healthy stage is in a positive, constructive, i.e., ethical relationship to his fellow men."[17] For Adler all the social context is the outcome of all behaviors. To understand the people and their interactions with one another is very important. Adler brings out a new theory of the Atonement focusing on 'Social context.' The person of God who contributes to our well being is important for humanity.[18] Adler quotes Whitehead's view of the 'great companion-the fellow sufferer who understands us,' and Robinson's view of 'the man for others' to support his views. We no longer speak about the warrior-God, but we speak about the suffering servant and faithful spouse. For Adler than power the love of God is important for atonement.[19]

3.1.3. Carl Jung

Carl Jung also indirectly brings out the concept of unconscious self in humans connected with Atonement. The shadow which is the dark side of a personality makes a person to feel inferior or unwanted. The forces of unconscious are dark, threatening and stormy.[20] Psychological healing will take place only when the unconscious made into consciousness. Therapist will bring back client's ego which he/she lost because of unconsciousness.[21] The dark and inferior sides become a good and wholeness. If we apply this in Atonement Christ came to bring reconciliation between God and humans. The darkness or sin is restored with salvation.

3.1.4. Carl Rogers

Carl Rogers focus on the client-centered vision of health and brokenness. He says that healing and brokenness are interdependent and from psychological point of view *cure* or *change* are needed and from theological point of view *salvation* or *redemption* are needed.[22] He brings out four theoretical constructs to elucidate the client-centered view of health, they are as follows: The actualization tendency, in this Organism is taken as a whole and this organism should have a actualization tendency to transcend the deficiency; the organismic valuing process, it deals with the experiences and feelings, these feelings contains the social and moral meanings and values; Congruence, it deals with the openness to the experiences the rigidity of self-concept can be over come through congruence; The need for positive regard, in this process positive personality development and change is achieved.[23] Through the above constructs therapist accepts the client's broken feelings and the value of the client's self.

> The therapist acceptance is unconditional and empathic as he helps the client fell through repressed feelings. The therapist's unconditional positive regard emerges as an active process of positively caring for what the client is feeling. Empathy emerges as a passive process of participating in and feeling with the experiencing of the client.[24]

3.2. Atonement through 'Psychological Sacrifices': Towards a Borderless Church

A borderless Church can be achieved through the satisfactory reparation and this reparation in a way helps us to reconcile ourselves with God and our neighbors and this reparation can be done through certain psychological sacrifices (sacrificing certain feelings and emotions). Few of them are as follows:

3.2.1. Fear

Soren Kierkegaard says that fear is a *"sympathetic antipathy and an antipathetic sympathy directed towards an indefinite cause and produced by nothing."*[25] Sigmund Freud describes that fear is the reaction of the ego to inner danger of a threatening self-consciousness.[26] Alfred Adler explains that the fear is a *"valid or invalid expectation of danger or a hallucination that the danger is approaching."*[27] Real threat of life will cause fear in everyone. "Fear is a rational reaction to an objective identifiable external danger, which may involve flight or attack in self-defense."[28] Fear is common in all living creature and it is experienced as unpleasant. Fear is an emotion of uneasiness that arises as a normal response to the perceived danger that may be real or imagined.[29] The Fear of crossing borders will pushes a person to live within the borders. Peter's denial in Luke 22:56-61 helps us to understand that Peter had the fear of crossing borders like fear of death, fear of physical and mental torture, fear of losing a happy life, fear of losing identity and image, fear of breaking societal rules and regulations and so on. Like Peter many of us are struck in the fear of violating certain societal restrictions and when there is a psychological sacrifice of fear then a reparation will takes place and that reparation will construct a Borderless Church.

3.2.2. Anger

Andrew Lester, *pastoral theologian* views "anger and fear always coupled together, anger is a response to threat to the self-hood (physical self, the social self and self-esteem). The threat produces anxiety, which in turn produces both fear and anger."[30] Carroll Saussy focuses on Erick Erickson's eight stages[31] of development and argues that anger is the inevitable by-product at each stage; anger can block the development of each stage. If the anger can be used positively, it supplies the energy needed to accomplish the challenge of each stage. The appropriate expression of anger helps for both autonomy and relation with others.[32] Psychiatrist Donald Nathanson defines that "anger is one of the unlearned primitive affects that become the basis of our emotional life."[33] However, anger is secondary emotion which follows primary emotions lie fear, frustration or hurt.[34] Ephesians 4:26 states that, "Be angry but so not sin; do not let the sun go down on your anger," here the negative anger is compared with sin. When we are crossing the Borders, we will be caught up with certain issues like jealousy towards other people, believing and justifying that our views are the only correct solutions, fear of breaking certain socio-religious, political and economic impositions and so on. When these expectations are scattered, we tend to experience anger in a very negative way and thereby it does not allow us to cross the borders. So, sacrificing the negative anger will point us towards the borderless Church.

3.2.3. *Low Self-Esteem*

Abraham Maslow, the American Psychologist says that, "The Esteem needs are the needs which focuses on self-respect/self-esteem and esteem from others."[35]

1. Self-respect/self-esteem deals with desire for strength, confidence, achievement, independence, freedom, competence and so on.

2. Esteem from others deals with prestige, recognition, acceptance, attention, status, reputation, appreciation, dignity and so on.

Gratification of these needs helps an individual to feel self-confident, strength, capable and necessary in the world but when these needs are failed then the individual develops a feeling of inferiority, weakness, hopelessness and helplessness; this will hurt an individual very badly.[36] Leviticus 13, 14 chapters charts down the symptoms of leprosy and how lepers should be treated. Lepers are considered as unclean and anyone who is in contact with the lepers will also be considered as unclean. When Jesus heals a leper in Mark 1:40-42, he very well knew that dealing with a leper will bring some damage to his self-esteem and thereby his prestige, recognition, identity, dignity and so on will be degraded. But Jesus decided to stick to his manifesto by not considering the concept of low self-esteem which will be pushed into his life. Likewise, when we want to cross the borders while dealing with the people infected and affected with AIDS, LGBTIQ and so on, we will be forced to face low Self-esteem, but we need to sacrifice the image of (low) self-esteem to create a borderless Church.

3.2.4. *Shame*

C.D. Schneider says that, Shame is a painful feeling of disgrace, dishonor, and of being exposed, uncovered, unprotected and vulnerable.[37] Shame can be an experience of an attack or humiliation. Some of the shame related experiences are embarrassment, humiliation, disgrace, dishonor, shyness, ridicule and so on. John 4:1-15 narrates the conversation between Jesus and the Woman of Samaria. There was a constant rift between Jews and Samaritans, Jews are not supposed to have any kind of relationship with Samaritans, Jews excommunicated and cursed them on several occasions.

The concept of Shame is attached to the Samaritans because of the vulnerability, embarrassment, humiliation, disgrace and dishonor which they face from Jews. If Jews eat anything that of Samaritan's, share things in common with Samaritans will also force to feel Shame. That's why when Jesus asked water, Samaritan woman replied, 'How is it that you, a Jew, ask a drink of me, a woman of Samaria? (v.9). But Jesus was ready to face the shame in order to break the borders of inferiority and superiority, borders of gender, borders of social and cultural impositions and so on. Likewise many times we need to face Shame if we go beyond social and cultural constructions and if we are ready to sacrifice the feeling of Shame (i.e. we no need to feel dishonored, disgraced when we work for the common humanity, charity and civility) then we can create a borderless Church which is free from caste, class, gender, power and so on.

4.   Conclusion

Borders do exist everywhere; Church cannot be exempted from that borders. Unfortunately, Church had adopted borders from many centuries. On one side, borders are identity makers and it reminds us about what we are and what we are becoming but on the other side these borders will force us to confine ourselves to a limited understanding of the Church, at this point of time the concept of borderless church emerges to create the powerful expression of oneness. In order to march towards the borderless Church, the inward engagement is essential. This inward engagement deals more with the healing of mind through psychological procedures. The psychological intervention of the theory of 'Atonement' acts as a channel to understand the borderless Church through healing of the mind.

Atonement is the redeeming work of Jesus Christ. Jesus Christ made satisfactory reparation to the sins of the humans through sacrificing himself on the cross. Through the Cross Christ brought salvation and reconciliation. One needs to understand Atonement considering faith, hope and love. Atonement process has the potency to heal us from our brokenness or strife and restores us with health and wholeness. The offense or injury which took place in the Church through borders can be altered with the satisfactory reparation/ amendment and this reparation can build the state of oneness and reconciliation. Psychological understanding of Atonement widens our cognitive capacities to move towards a borderless Church through sacrificing certain feelings and emotions such as fear, anger, low self-esteem, shame, guilt and so on. In order to affirm the process of being and becoming a Christ community, borderless Church is required, and this borderless Church can be achieved through the healing of mind. Healing of mind can be achieved through various procedures among which psychological practice of Atonement plays a vital role.

Endnotes

[1] Robert S. Paul, *The Atonement and the Sacraments* (Nashville: Abingdon Press, 1960), 20.

[2] "(Literally, a setting at one). The state of, or act of bringing into, concord; restoration of friendly relations; reconciliation. That means the condition of being at one with others; unity of feeling, harmony, concord and agreement. In Theology, atonement means the saving of redeeming work of Christ wrought through his incarnation, sufferings, and death; also, reconciliation between God and men, especially as effected by Christ." Robert S. Paul, *The Atonement and the Sacraments...*, 18.

[3] Edward Grubb, *The Meaning of the Cross: A Study of the Atonement* (London: George Allen & Unwin Ltd, 1922), 28.

[4] https://www.academia.edu/10581867/A_Biblical_Understanding_of_Christs_Atonement, accessed on 4/09/2018.

[5] Lev 17:11 says that, "for the life of the flesh is in the blood; and I have given it to you for making atonement for your lives on the altar; for, as life, it is the blood that makes atonement." NRSV

[6] Charles E Hill, "Atonement in the Old Testament and New Testaments," in *The Glory of the Atonement*, edited by Charles E. Hill and Frank A. James III (Illinois: InterVarsity Press: 2004), 25.

[7] Substitutionary offering of the righteous servant is required to save the unfaithful Israelites. J.K. Mozley, *The Doctrine of the Atonement* (London: Gerald Duckworth & Co. Ltd., 1953), 27,28

[8] Micah 6:6-8, Hosea 6:6 says that, 'For I desire steadfast love and not sacrifice.' Jeremiah 31:31-34 also says about new covenant by rejecting old covenant of sacrifices.

[9] J.K. Mozley, *The Doctrine of the Atonement...*, 24.

[10] Edward Grubb, *The Meaning of the Cross: A Study of the Atonement...*, 50.

[11] Royce Gordon Gruenler, "Atonement in the Synoptic Gospels and Acts," in *The Glory of the Atonement...*, 94.

[12] Edward Grubb, *The Meaning of the Cross: A Study of the Atonement...*, 59

[13] Royce Gordon Gruenler, "Atonement in the Synoptic Gospels and Acts," in *The Glory of the Atonement...*, 97.

[14] Sigmund Freud, *Moses and Monotheism* (New York: Vintage Books, 1939), 148,149.

[15] Sigmund Freud, *Totem and Taboo* (New York: W.W.Norton & Company Inc., 1950), 2-4.

[16] Sigmund Freud, *Totem and Taboo...*, 20.

[17] Richard C. Erickson, "Social Interest: Relating Adlerian Psychology to Christian Theology," *Pastoral Psychology* 32/2 (Winter, 1983): 131.

[18] Richard C. Erickson, "Social Interest...," 131.

[19] Richard C. Erickson, "Social Interest...," 136,137.

[20] John A.Sanford, *Healing and Wholeness* (New York: Paulist Press, 1977), 92.

[21] John A.Sanford, *Healing and Wholeness...*, 94.

[22] Don S. Browning, *Atonement and Psychotherapy* (Philadelphia: The Westminister Press, 1966) 96.

[23] Don S. Browning, *Atonement and Psychotherapy...*, 96-103.

[24] Ralph E.James, "A Theology of Acceptance," *The Journal of Religion* 49/4 (October, 1969): 378.

[25] Oscar Pfister, *Christianity and Fear: A Study in History and in the Psychology and Hygiene of Religion* (London: George Allen & Unwin Ltd, 1948), 46-48.

[26] Oscar Pfister, *Christianity and Fear...*, 49-51.

[27] Oscar Pfister, *Christianity and Fear...*,52.

[28] L.Wright, "Fear," *Dictionary of Pastoral Care and Counseling*, edited by Rodney J. Hunter (Bangalore: TPI, 2007), 430.

[29] Oscar Pfister, *Christianity and fear ...*, 41.

[30] Carroll Saussy, *The Gift of Anger: A Call to Faithful Action* (Louisville: Westminster John Knox Press, 1995), 15.

[31] 1). Trust versus mistrust (infancy); 2). Autonomy versus shame or doubt (early childhood); 3). Initiative versus guilt (play age); 4). Industry versus inferiority (school age); 5). Identity versus identity diffusion (adolescence); 6). Intimacy versus isolation (young adulthood); 7). Generativity versus self-absorption (adulthood); and 8). Integrity versus despair (old age). Carroll Saussy, *The Gift of Anger...*, 41.

[32] Donald Capps, "Pastoral Care and the Eight Deadly Vices," *Pastoral Psychology* 32/1 (fall, 1983): 8, 9.

[33] In other words we no need to learn anger, the affect followed very early experiences where in our needs were not met. For ex: Frustration-sometimes child wants the people who takes out, if father/mother does not take child out then child develops dislike on father/mother, if father/mother embraces child then child tend to cry, so child develops attitude of expressing emotion when she/he does not like anything and this might be anger or it might develop into anger. Paula Caplan, *Don't blame Mother* (NewYork: Harper & Row, 1989), 25, cited by Carroll Saussy, *The Gift of Anger...*, 28.

[34] Mark S. Jones, "Anger and Personality Disorders," *The Journal of Pastoral Care* 51/1 (1997): 91, 92.

[35] Frank G. Goble, *The Third Force: The Psychology of Abraham Maslow* (New York: Pocket Books, 1970), 42.

[36] Abraham H Maslow, *Motivation and Personality,* 3rd ed (Delhi: Pearson Education, Inc., 1987), 21.

[37] C.D. Schneider, "Shame," *Dictionary of Pastoral Care and Counseling..*, 1160.

Contributors

1. Dr. Daniel Ezhilarasu, Rtd. Principal, Voorhees College.

2. Dr. S. Angelin Sheeja, Assistant Professor in English, Nesamony Memorial Christian College, Marthandam.

3. Rev. Dr. P. Bethel Krupa Victor, Faculty, UTC.

4. Dr. Kamala D. Dhawale, Principal, CSI College of Commerce Dharwad, Karnataka.

5. Dr. Mini Chacko, Vice Principal & Associate Professor, CMS College Kottayam, Kerala.

6. Dr. Mrs. V. Regina, Principal, CSI Bishop Newbigin College of Education, Chennai.

7. Dr. A. Umesh Samuel Jebaseelan, Dean (R&D) & Associate Professor in Social Work, Bishop Heber College, Trichy.

8. Mr. Jacob Swamynathan, Entrepreneur, Skill Factory.

9. Rev. C.R. Vincent, Resource person for 'CHRISTIAN EDUCATION', Part-time faculty of KUTS, Kannammoola, TVPM, Presbyter-in-charge and District Chairman,CSI Kattakada,SKD.

10. Rev. Dr. T. I. James, Vicar, CSI Cathedral, CSI Diocese of Malabar

11. Dr. Mrs. Thayalini Thiagarajah, President Women's Fellowship, CSI Diocese in Jaffna, Srilanka.

12. Rev. Dr. Arul Dhas T., Chaplain, Christian Medical College, Vellore.

13. Rev. Dr. A. Israel David, Associate professor, Pastoral Counselling. Faculty Dean (Academic) and Dean of Doctoral Programmes, Union Biblical Seminary, Pune.

14. At present serving as Presbyter in Nellaraikonam Pastorate Church, CSI Kanyakumari Diocese. Previously I was teaching at United Theological College in the Department of Religion and Culture. I completed my research period in Gurukul Lutheran Theological College & Research Institute, submitted my D.TH thesis and waiting for the result.

15. Dr. Samson Gandhi, Executive Director, Person to Person - Institute for Christian Counselling.

16. Dr. Sheela Noone, Gynecologist, CSI Malabar Diocese.

17. Rev. Sharath Sowseelya, Presbyter, CSI Rayalaseema Diocese.

18. Mr. Livingstone Arputharaj, Assistant Professor, Gurukul Lutheran Theological College and Research Institute, Chennai.

19. Rev. Sudhir Karunakar, Presbyter, CSI Karimnagar Diocese.

20. Rev Dr Samuel Jayakumar, PhD (OCMS, Oxford), Director, Evangelical Theological Academy, Chennai.

21. Rev. John Nischal, Presbyter, CSI Rayalaseema Diocese.

www.ingramcontent.com/pod-product-compliance
Lightning Source LLC
LaVergne TN
LVHW091701190726
843493LV00001B/101